A selection of

WILDFLOWERS
OF SOUTHERN SPAIN

Betty Molesworth Allen

Wildflowers of Southern Spain is published by Ediciones Santana. S.L., Apartado 422 - 29640 Fuengirola (Málaga) Spain. Telephone 952 48 58 38. Fax 952 48 53 67. E-mail: santana@vnet.es

First published in April 1993
Reprinted in July 2000

ISBN: 84-89954-12-7   Depósito Legal: M-23.536/1987

In appreciation to the late Diana Brinton-Lee who shared her wide knowledge of southern Spanish flowers with me.

CONTENTS

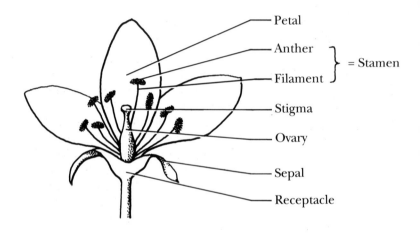

Petal

Anther

Filament

} = Stamen

Stigma

Ovary

Sepal

Receptacle

INTRODUCTION

In this book I have tried to give easy indentifications with simple text to some of the common wildflowers of southern Andalusia (covering the latitude approximately 36 - 36.5)

Even in this relatively small area of southern Spain there is an enormous diversity of wildflowers in various habitats from coastal plains to high mountains. Of course, many of the plants are found in other Mediterranean countries, but there are also endemics, plants that occur nowhere else, and a small overlap from North Africa gives even greater botanical richness.

From April through to late June, fields of yellow, purple, red and white flowers, mainly annuals, hasten through their floral cycles before summer heat and drought burns up the countryside. Others, perennials, tend to linger and, of course, those by streams and ponds may flower much longer. In fact there are flowers to be found all the year round, for in the high mountains the season is from late June to August then autumn bulbs start blooming in the lowlands from September. The Small Pheasant's Eye Narcissus (page 203) covers sandy fields in a profusion of blossoms followed by Crocuses, Colchicum and the endemic Green Narcissus, Scillas and other bulbs. From about November or December, usually after much rain, the Paper-white Narcissus (page 202) in low-lying damp fields, brightens the dull days of winter with huge patches of its pure white flowers.

Winter on the whole is mild and wet, but temperatures even in the lowlands occasionally drop to freezing for a short time and frosts may occur in the southwest. Snow lies a few times a year on the summits of hills as low as 2-3,000 feet (600-900 metres) from about the Sierra Bermeja eastwards. By February the sun is strong enough to bring out spring flowers until the ground dries out about early July, bringing high temperatures for the next few months.

Vegetation varies a great deal between the southwest corner and the eastern Costa del Sol. For instance, from the west to about Sotogrande, apart from the Jurassic limestone outcrop of Gibraltar, soils are predominately tertiary sandstone, neutral to acid. Much of the hilly land is covered with heathlands and corkwoods; in the arable plains are cultivations of seasonal crops and cattle farms.

Large areas of this yellowish soil are covered with the evergreen Cork Oak (*Quercus suber*) mixed with about five species of deciduous oaks (*Quejigo*) and their hybrids. The floor is usually covered with tall Bracken Fern (*Pteridum aquilinum*), and on river and stream banks are Holly (*Ilex aquifolium*), Narrow-leaved Ash (*Fraxinus angustifolia*) and Common Alder (*Alnus glutinosa*) simulating woods of a cooler climate. Mixed with these, however, are the wild pink-flowered Rhododendron (R. *ponticum* ssp. *baeticum*), which is still fairly common from about 80-670 m. in altitude and flowering about April.

On open rocky hills and low country, heathlands may comprise Ling (*Calluna* page 107) with several species of Heather forming a dominant association amongst Wild Olive, Lentisc, Kermes Oak (Q. *coccifera*) and the Dwarf Palm (*Chamaerops humilis*).

Large farms are scattered over the countryside, some breed black bulls for the bullring, others have herds of the ancient breed of dark red cattle, the Retinto. During the last two decades, however, white Chareolet cattle from France have been imported, resulting in pale *cafe-au-lait* animals amongst the Retinto.

Commonly grown are crops of Wheat, Oats, Sugarbeet, Chickpeas, Maize and colourful fields of Sunflowers. Most of this changes, however, as one travels eastwards from about Sotogrande to the Costa del Sol. Limestone hills, often of the same formation as Gibraltar, become common, cattle and heathlands rare. Groves of cultivated Olives, Citrus, Grapes and Figs are frequently seen. Large plantations of Spanish Chestnuts and Almonds are cultivated east of Gaucin, with Cherry orchards in some of the valleys. Around here, and towards Grazalema and Ronda, small pockets of neutral soil occur, which are usually indicated by the presence of Cork Oaks and the sticky white-flowered *Cistus* shrub (page 88). Crops are also cultivated in some of the valleys.

The coastal strip, once covered with early spring wildflowers, is now mainly built over and a new plant association has appeared through lavish planting of tropical and sub-tropical flowering trees and shrubs. The climate in this coastal strip is usually warmer in winter than in the southwest, as it is protected from most cold winds by the high mountains behind it.

From the town of Estepona a road winds up an interesting mountain to about 3,000 feet (900 metres). It is the Sierra Bermeja (Los Reales) and consists mainly of a volcanic rock called peridotite on which many plants grow that are rare elsewhere. It is also the easiest place to see the unique Spanish Fir (*Abies pinsapo*) which is now found in the wild only in three places.

All through southern Spain good roads lead to open country where wildflowers are still abundant. In the extreme southwest is the famous National Park of Donaña – a rich area for wildflowers as well as for birds and animals.

A few miles inland from Gibraltar and Algeciras, roads to Jerez and Seville run through open country, and from April to May roadsides and fields are covered with flowers, a wonderful sight in this overcrowded and built-up world.

From the Costa del Sol there are many roads leading inland to mountainous country and behind Marbella is the Sierra Blanca Reserve, where Spanish Ibex may be seen as well as very interesting wildflowers.

From Malaga it is an easy run to Granada from where a road climbs up the Sierra Nevada to about 10,000 feet (3,000 metres) Here, on the high slopes, flowering is best between July and August where there are good examples of "Hedgehog Zone" plants. Mainly low and dense, often spiny and growing close together, they have become adapted to withstand the searing winds and freezing temperatures of these high altitudes.

Most of the areas mentioned in the text are now private land, reserves or national parks where plants may not be picked. So please leave the flowers for others to enjoy and use a camera instead to record what you have seen.

Flowering times given in the text are only an indication, since so much depends on climate, soil and altitude. Finally, to keep the book small enough to carry easily, I have had to omit many plants I would like to have included, but have tried to give examples of common species within a family.

BOTANICAL NOTE

In this book I have followed the order of the plants used in *Flora Europaea*, Vols 1-5 (1964-1980); T. G. Tutin and others, Cambridge University Press.

Since the publication of this book there have been some name changes in a more recent and excellent publication on western Spain: *Flora Vascular de Andalucia Occidentale*, 3 vols. (1987) B. Valdes & others. These name changes are in brackets alongside the older name.

It is often annoying, especially to a non-botanist, to find that a plant you know by a certain name is suddenly called something else. This, unfortunately, has become necessary, as in the past when plants were given names there was often little communication between the nearby countries where overlaps of species occurred. This resulted in different names being given to one species, especially between France, Italy and Spain where there is similar vegetation.

There are also some old families that have retained the spelling ending in AE which Carl Linnaeus, the great Swedish botanist, used in his 1764 publications. These are now being brought into line and tend to be used in modern works.

PLANT GUIDE BY FLOWER COLOUR

Predominately White

Herbs - annual or perennial, not woody

Allium ampeloprasum, large, bulb, onion - also pink
A. nigrum, large, bulb, onion - also pink
Acanthus mollis, perennial, tall erect
Ammi majus, carrot, tall
A. visnaga, carrot, tall
Anterrhinum granaticum, Snapdragon, perennial
Arenaria tetraquetra, perennial, low, mountains
Asphodelus albus, lily, tubers, tall
Bellis annua, daisy, small
B. perennis, daisy, perennial
B. sylvestris, daisy, perennial
Cerastium boissieri, perennial, low
Chaenorhinum villosum, also pink, rocks
Chamaemelum fuscatum, daisy, annual, early spring
Conium maculatum, carrot, spotted stems
Daucus carota, carrot, stems not spotted
Helianthemum appenninum, low, mountains
Iberis crenata, Candytuft, flat heads
Leucojum trichophyllum, small, bulb, tinged pink
Linaria amethystea, annual, small, white/pink
Linum suffruticosum, often red eye
Lobularia maritima, small, flowers in heads
Narcissus papyraceus, bulb, autumn
N. serotinus, small, bulb, coloured eye, autumn
Omphalodes brassicifolia, small, annual
Pancratium maritimum, bulb, large, sand
Paronychia echinata, low, shiny bracts
Saxifraga boissieri, rocks, mountains
S. globulifera, lowlands and mountains
Teucrium scorodonia, perennial, to pale cream
Urginea maritima, bulb, leafless at flowering

Shrubs, perennial, woody branches

Capparis ovata, spiny
Cistus ladanifer, sticky leaves

C. salvifolius, small, rough leaves
Erica arborea, tall, heather
Myrtus communis, to small tree
Prasium majus, small, shiny leaves
Rosa sempervirens, weak stems

Climbers

Clematis cirrhosa, drooping flowers

Cream to Green

Herbs, annual or perennial, not woody

Plantago lagopus, basal leaves
Sedum sediforme, fleshy, flowers green
Silene andryalifolia, sticky, cream
Stachys ocymastrum, small, cream

Shrubs, perennial, woody branches

Daphne gnidium, cream
D. laureola, green
Erica scoparia, green or pinkish

Trees

Arbutus unedo, cream
Olea europaea, olive, cream
Viscum cruciatum, parasite on trees, green

Climbers

Clematis cirrhosa, cream or white to green

Predominately Yellow

Herbs, annual or perennial, not woody

Ajuga chamaepitys, small pine-like leaves
Alyssum serpyphyllum, rounded bush
Anacyclus radiatus, daisy
Anemone palmata, basal leaves
Andryala integrifolia, daisy, soft leaves
Arctotheca calendula, daisy, cream/yellow
Asteriscus maritimus, daisy, coastal
Biscutella frutescens, perennial, tall, mountains
Bupleurum lancifolium, annual, small
Calendula suffruticosa, daisy

Chrysanthemum coronarium, daisy, cream/yellow
Digitalis obscura, yellow/brown
Dittrichia viscosa, daisy, sticky leaves
Doronicum plantagineum, daisy, mountains
Ecballium elaterium, cucumber, pale
Euphorbia nicaeensis, milky juice
Ferula communis, carrot, biennial, tall
Helichrysum stoechas, heads, yellow bracts
Linaria spartea, annual, one stem, slender
Lotus creticus, perennial, low
Narcissus bulbocodium, Hoop Daffodil
Oxalis pes-caprae, small clover leaves
Phlomis lychnitis, pale hairy leaves, mountains
Ranunculus bullatus, basal leaves, autumn
R. ficaria, large, sepals 3, spring
Reichardia gaditana, daisy, dark eye
Scorzonera crispatula, daisy, dark eye
Sedum acre, fleshy leaves, small
S. tenuifolium, fleshy leaves
Sternbergia lutea, bulb
Thapsia garganica, carrot, tall
Tolpis barbata, daisy, dark eye
Tulipa sylvestris, red/yellow petals
Verbascum pulverulentum, branched, tall
V. sinuatum, branched

Shrubs, perennial, woody branches
Adenocarpus telonensis, Broom, pod glandular
Bupleurum fruticosum, leaf-veins netted
Calicotome villosa, Broom, spiny
Coronilla valentina, hairless, pea flowers
Cytisus baeticus, Broom, whippy branches, tall
C. grandiflorus, Broom, whippy branches, tall
Dittrichia viscosa, sticky, small
Genista cinerea, Broom, mountains
G. hirsuta, Broom, spiny, hairy
G. linifolia, Broom, flowers in heads
G. tridens, Broom, spiny

Halimium halimifolium, Rockrose, grey leaves
Ononis natrix, Restharrow, sticky
O. speciosa, Restharrow, lupin-like heads
Retama sphaerocarpa, Broom, whippy branches
Ulex parviflorus, Gorse, spiny

Thistles
Carlina racemosa, annual, branched, small
Carthamnus arborescens, shrub, large
Scolymus hispanicus, perennial, branched

Trees without petals
Pistacia lentiscus, shrub to tree
P. terebinthus, large shrub to tree

Red and Yellow

Herbs - annual or perennial, not woody
Cytinus hypocistus, parasite, base of shrubs
Tulipa sylvestris, bulb, small

Orange to Red

Herbs - annual or perennial, not woody
Hedysarum coronarium, low, crimson
Orobanche haensleri, Broomrape, parasite
Papaver rhoeas, Common Poppy, annual
Tetragonolobus purpurea, annual, deep red

Predominately Pink - Pale to Dark

Herbs - annual or perennial, not woody
Allium nigrum, bulb, onion, also white
Anterrhinum majus, perennial
Centaurea pullata, Knapweed, perennial, low
Centaurium erythraea, biennial, small, erect
Colchicum lusitanicum, bulb, checkered, autumn
Crocus serotinus, bulb, small, not checkered, autumn
Chaenorhinum villosum, pink and purple
Dianthus hispanicus, very narrow leaves
Digitalis purpurea, Foxglove, tall

Dipsacus fullonum, robust, prickly
Echium albicans, hairy, erect
E. boissieri, tall head
Erodium primulaceum, annual, small
Fedia cornucopia, annual, low
Frankenia laevis, perennial, mat forming
Geranium malviflorum, perennial, small, soft
Leucojum trichophyllum, small, white/pink
Leuzia conifera, like soft pine-cone, small
Linaria amethystea, annual, small, white/pink
Lythrum junceum, small, damp
L. salicaria, tall, damp
Malope malacoides, Mallow
Malva sylvestris, Mallow, biennial
Paeonia broteri, large flowers, hills
Pistorinia hispanicus, annual, small, fleshy
Putoria calabrica, cliffs, hills
Romulea bulbocodium, bulb, small
R. clusiana, bulb, coastal sands
Salvia sclarea, biennial, robust
Silene psammitis, annual, small, sticky
Spergularia rubra, slender, almost flat
Thymus granatensis, low, mountains

Thistles

Chamaeleon gummifer, perennial, stemless
Cirsium echinatum, mountains
C. scabrum, very tall, lowlands
Galactites tomentosa, annual, variegated leaves
Ptilostemon hispanicus, perennial, mountains
Silybum marianum, mottled shiny leaves

Shrubs, perennial, woody branches

Cistus albidus, grey leaves
C. crispus, green leaves
Erica australis, flowers December-June
E. ciliaris, flowers large, August-October
E. umbellata, small, February-June
Lavatera maritima, very pale pink

Lonicera arborea, pink/cream
Nerium oleander, open streamsides
Phlomis purpurea, grey leaves
Prunus prostrata, flat, woody, mountains
Thymus capitatus, Thyme

Climbers

Convolvulus althaeoides, also on ground

Predominately Lilac to Purple

Herbs - annual or perennial, not woody

Arisarum vulgare, Arum, small, hooded purplish
Calamintha sylvatica, aromatic, lilac
Campanula mollis, lilac to almost blue
C. specularioides, lilac
Cerinthe major, annual, tubular flowers
Chaenorhinum villosum, to almost white
Delphinium nanum, annual, purplish
D. staphisagria, annual, violet, sticky
Dipsacus fullonum, spiny
Echium plantagineum, annual, hairy
Galega officinalis, lilac/white, damp
Geranium malviflorum, pink to purplish
Gynandiris sisyrinchium, Iris, small, fine leaves
Iris planifolia, small, wide leaves
I. filifolia, tall, purple
Lythrum junceum, small, damp
Mandragora autumnalis, stemless, autumn
Mentha pulegium, Mint
Polygala microphylla, small, few leaves
Romulea bulbocodium, bulb, stemless
Thymus capitatus, woody, pink to lilac
Trachelium caeruleum, flat heads

Shrubs, perennial, woody branches

Erinacea anthyllis, Broom, mountains
Lavandula dentata, toothed leaves
L. multifida, shrublet, leaves pinnate
L. stoechas, flowers with pink topknots

Rosmarinus officinalis, leaves dark green above
Teucrium fruticans, leaves greyish
Thymus capitatus, Thyme
Vitex agnus-castus, to small tree, lilac

Climbers

Aristolochia baetica, purple
Lathyrus tingitana, reddish-purple

Predominately Blue to Violet-Blue

Herbs - annual or perennial, not woody

Anagallis monelli, small, sand
Anchusa azurea, annual, hairy
Borago officinalis, Borage
Campanula mollis, to lilac
Delphinium nanum, violet/blue
Echium plantagineum, to lilac
Eryngium dilatatum, very spiny
Iris xiphium, tall, bluish
Linum narbonense, Flax, large flowers
Lithodora fruticosa, hairy, occasionally woody
Lupinus micranthus, annual, sand
Mandragora officinalis, lilac/blue
Polygala microphylla, few leaves
Scilla peruviana, very large bulb
Vinca difformis, Periwinkle, low

Shrubs, perennial, woody branches

Lithodora fruticosa, occasionally woody

Orchids - Mixed Colours

Anacamptis pyramidalis, mainly pink
Barlia robertiana, very tall, scented, pink
Himantoglossum hircinum, tall, long thin lobes
Orphrys scolopax, pink and purplish
Orchis coriophora, scented, mainly pink/white
O. italica, pink, "little men" shapes

***VISCUM CRUCIATUM*, Red-berried Mistletoe,** Marojo, Muérdago.

Description: A partial-parasitic plant with open branches living on medium-sized trees and shrubs. Leaves smooth, thick and hairless, pale green and in opposite pairs on the twigs; veins parallel 3-7. Flowers small, green in clumps of about 3-9, male flowers with stamens, falling rapidly; female flowers developing into round berries, green then ripening bright red, translucent and very sticky.

Flowering: Berries ripening from December to about April.

Habitat: Parasitic mainly on wild olive trees, but also on Hawthorn (*Crataegus* spp.) in the mountains and on a few other trees and shrubs. In rocky and limestone areas.

Distribution: Southern Spain, Portugal, North Africa, usually above 500m in our area.

Family: Mistletoe family, Loranthaceae (Viscaceae).

Notes: The white berried *Viscum album* is rare here if it does come into our area. Having green leaves they are only partially parasitic, but can kill the host if there are many plants on it. Birds eat the sticky berries then wipe their bills on branches thus transferring the seeds. Mistletoe was called the Golden Bough by the Roman poet Virgil, and strange powers are attributed to it.

ARISTOLOCHIA BAETICA, **Dutchman's Pipe,** Candiles, Aristoloquia bética.

Description: Very robust, tall hairless creeper; rather thick pliable stems clambering high into trees, shrubs or along the ground.   Leaves dull, blue-green and heart-shaped.   Flowers about 7cm long, curved, dull red-purple to brownish-red. Capsules pendant, oblong, green at first ripening black and dry, then splitting into 6 valves.   Seeds about 5mm, flat.

Flowering: Over a long period from autumn to early spring.

Habitat: Almost any soil; semi-shade in thickets and on edges of woods, streamsides.   Usually low altitudes, replaced by other species in the mountains.   Most abundant in the west.

Distribution: Southern and eastern Spain, southern Portugal, North Africa.

Family: Dutchman's Pipe family, Aristolochiaceae.

Notes: Roots have been used in Spain since at least the 16th century for reducing fever. Other species also contain medicinal properties. Used in the past for snake-bites and abortion. There are several species of *Aristolochia* in southern Spain. A. *paucinervis* (old name *longa*) is a small spreading herb with pale green leaves and yellow-green flowers. In light cork woods and in open places in the east.

CYTINUS HYPOCISTIS, **Doncella,** Hipocisto.

Description: Low growing perennial parasite with a very short stem about 9-10cm high. There are no green leaves (no chlorophyll); it gets its nourishment from the roots of other plants. Flowers are yellow surrounded by scarlet overlapping scale-leaves.

Flowering: March to early July.

Habitat: Growing on roots of *Cistus* at the bases of stems on several species and on *Halimium* as well. Common in southern Spain.

Distribution: Mediterranean, Portugal, North Africa.

Family: A tropical parasitic family, Rafflesiaceae.

Notes: Conspicuous in flower, large plants may be 16-20cm across, by then the host plant usually shows that it is being drained of its food. Belongs to the same family as the Sumatran *Rafflesia arnoldi*, which has the largest flower in the world, almost one metre across and practically stemless. It is parasitic on vines in forests, is dull red and has a terrible smell, attracting flies and other insects for pollination. In the past, fresh juice of Cytinus was used in medicine by the Greeks, at least as long ago as the 2nd Centuary AD (Dioscorides in his *Materia Medica*).

ARENARIA TETRAQUETRA, **Mountain Sandwort,** Arenária.

Description: Compact perennial herb not more than 30cm high, usually less. Leaves closely imbricated into rosettes of four, forming dense cushions; leaves tough in texture, small and not more than 5mm long with recurved tips. Flowers with 4-5 petals, white, solitary; many out at one time.

Flowering: About July to September.

Habitat: Dry and often sloping rocky ground, or in rubble on exposed places on mountains from over 1,500m.

Distribution: France and Spain (Pyrenees); southern Spanish mountains, especially on the Sierra Nevada.

Family: Carnation family, Caryophyllaceae.

Notes: Another similar species with which it could be confused is A. *aggregata*. It has sharp-pointed leaf tips and appears to start flowering later.

***CERASTIUM BOISSIERI*, Chickweed.**

Description: Low growing perennial, about 10-30cm high, spreading and forming rather loose patches. Leaves about 2cm long, narrow and pointed, sometimes recurved, usually greyish. Flowers about 2-3cm across; flower-stems, sepals and bracts with glandular hairs.

Flowering: April to July.

Habitat: Rocky dry places, in rubble and earth especially in limestone areas, and in broken ground amongst small xerophytic shrubs; hills and mountains mainly.

Distribution: In southern Spain, very common in the higher hills and mountains to high altitudes. Rare in Corsica and Sardinia; North Africa.

Family: Carnation family, Caryophyllaceae.

Notes: Replaced in Gibraltar by the almost identical C. *gibraltaricum* which is considered by some botanists to belong to the above species. They are closely related to the cultivated Chickweed.

DIANTHUS HISPANICUS, **Pink,** Clavellinas.

Description: Rather slender, tufted perennial with stems about 30-40cm long, seldom branched. Leaves short and narrow often recurved; usually paired on stems. Flowers about 1.5-2cm wide, petals without a beard (hairs); usually scentless.

Flowering: July to September.

Habitat: Dry open places, rock crevices, grassy sloping ground by rocks in hills and mountains.

Distribution: Spain and southern France.

Family: Carnation family, Caryophyllaceae.

Notes: Southern Spain has several species of *Dianthus* which may be difficult to distinguish, but a conspicuous one from our area which has long fringed petals and a strong scent is *D.broteri,* which used to be common in limestone areas in both lowlands and high hills.

PARONYCHIA CAPITATA, **Paronychia**, Arrecadas.

Description: Small branched perennial herb, low growing, about 15cm high. Leaves very small, hairy and sharp-pointed; hidden under the flowering bracts. Flowers tiny, in clusters amongst the conspicuous heads of silvery-white bracts.

Flowering: From about May with a long flowering period when the bracts are conspicuous, remaining until August when the plant is in seed, and the bracts gradually becoming dull and falling.

Habitat: Nearly always in hills and mountains on bare limestone rocks or amongst sand or stony rubble on roadsides below cliffs.

Distribution: Most Mediterranean countries, frequent in southern Spain.

Family: Carnation family, Caryophyllaceae.

Notes: Spectacular when the bracts glisten in the sun. Common near Grazalema and on the hills behind Marbella. Some other species of *Paronychia* have been used in medicine.

SILENE ANDRYALIFOLIA, **Mountain Catchfly.**

Description: Perennial with sticky (glandular) hairs on calyx and stalks. Leaves pointed and tufted at the bases of flowering stalks. Flowers, about 2cm diameter, cream with each petal deeply cut into lobes; calyx, long narrow and hairy, with 10 veins.

Flowering: About early May to July.

Habitat: Essentially a rock plant growing in clumps in crevices, often on bare vertical cliffs.

Distribution: Southern Spain, not elsewhere in Europe, but occuring in Morocco.

Family: Carnation family, Caryophyllaceae.

Notes: Alternative name: S.*pseudovelutina.* Commonly seen on limestone hills and mountains behind the Costa del Sol and around Grazalema. Is replaced in the non-limestone southwest by another glandular species, S. *nutans.* Also a crevice-lover, it has smaller, drooping flowers almost white, and comparatively wide leaves.

SILENE PSAMMITIS, **Sticky Catchfly,** Silene.

Description: Annual, glandular-hairy with spreading stems to about 20cm. Leaves narrow, sticky, about 1-3cm long. Flowers less than 2cm across, occasionally white; calyx with 10 veins, contracted at tip and widening in fruit. Seeds wingless.

Flowering: April to July.

Habitat: In stony ground, coarse sand (marble and slate association); mainly hills and mountains.

Distribution: Spain, Portugal.

Family: Carnation family, Caryophyllaceae.

Notes: Flowers open in sunshine. There are many *Silene* species in our area, most being difficult to identify, but this one is fairly distinct.

SPERGULARIA RUBRA, **Red Spurrey,** Vermella.

Description: Slender short-lived perennial or annual forming a fairly loose clump; plant variable in shape and size. Leaves very narrow in clusters subtended by papery sharp-pointed stipules. Flowers also with stipules at the base of the flowering stalk; flowers when fully open are about 1cm wide or less; sepals slightly shorter than the petals, but this varies; capsule a little longer or equalling the sepals, seeds unwinged, dark brown.

Flowering: January to June.

Habitat: Common in open sandy places, cultivated fields, in soft soils on roadsides. From lowlands to hills.

Distribution: Europe, North Africa, common in southern Spain.

Family: Carnation family, Caryophyllaceae.

Notes: In our area there are two fairly distinct subspecies which are most conspicuous when in full flower. The ssp. *longipes,* the commoner here, in the plate above, is slightly more lax with fewer flowers.

ANEMONE PALMATA, **Palmate Anemone,** Hierba centella.

Description: Small tuberous herb. Leaves mid green, often tinged with pink underneath; basal leaves about 5-7cm across or more, round in outline but margins shallowly cut into wide lobes; stem leaves stalkless cut into 3-5 linear segments. Flowers about 4-5cm across, shiny and frequently with red on the underside, softly hairy; flowering stems to 30cm but commonly between 15-20cm.

Flowering: February to May, June in the hills.

Habitat: Very common amongst low growth in heathlands, open woods in dry or damp places, lowlands to mountains.

Distribution: Southwest Europe, mainly Mediterranean.

Family: Buttercup family, Ranunculaceae.

Notes: In the past was used in Spanish country medicine as a poultice, but is a dangerous plant to use.

CLEMATIS CIRRHOSA, **December Clematis,** Virgin's Bower.

Description: Strong, high clambering plant growing over trees to at least 10m, but more conspicuously flowering on the tops of small trees and shrubs. Leaves variable, margins shallowly lobed. Flowers large, about 5cm long, drooping, greenish-cream to nearly white with a large green bract *(involucre)* on the stalk by the flower.

Flowering: November to January, but the conspicuous pale green and feathery seedheads, looking like flowers at a distance, remain at least until the end of March.

Habitat: Mainly over thickets of brambles, bushes, hedges and trees, and in the mountains over deciduous shrubs. All kinds of soils.

Distribution: Most of Mediterranean Europe, Portugal, all through our area of southern Spain.

Family: Buttercup family, Ranunculaceae.

Notes: Attractive when in flower and seed, but in the summer the leaves die, turning chaff-coloured and remaining on the plant which then becomes rather unsightly.

DELPHINIUM NANUM, **Annual Delphinium,** Espuela.

Description: Slender annual with widely spreading thin branches from an equally thin erect main-stalk; often branched again, height to about 70cm. Leaves at first basal, others 3-lobed but almost absent on flowering stems or dead by then; very small narrow and pointed, 1-3 lobed, lobes about 2mm wide. Flowers few with very short hairs on the spur. Seeds in erect capsules (follicles) splitting open into 3 parts.

Flowering: June to October.

Habitat: Scattered throughout from coastal sands to mountains; uncultivated fields, dry heathlands, edges of woods, mainly in loose soil.

Distribution: Spain, North Africa.

Family: Buttercup family, Ranunculaceae.

Notes: An earlier name is D. *obcordatum*. An uninspiring plant which is easily overlooked but it flowers when little else is out and occurs throughout our area.

DELPHINIUM STAPHISAGRIA, **Stavesacre,** Albarrara, Estafisagria.

Description: Erect, one-stemmed annual, rarely biennial; usually less than 1m high with long, thin and sticky hairs. Leaves pale green, large and almost circular in outline but deeply cut into irregular sharp-pointed lobes. Flowers in a terminal head varying in colour from a violet to a deep violet-blue; the spur at the back of the flower very short. Fruit in threes, chaff-coloured sharp-pointed and inflated, splitting on the inner side; covered with short, very sticky glandular hairs. Seeds black.

Flowering: May to June, July in mountains.

Habitat: In semi-shade preferring limestone; growing in stands in good soil, bases of cliffs in the hills but in the lowlands nearly always near rivers.

Distribution: Mediterranean area, Portugal. In southern Spain most commonly in hills and the lower mountains.

Family: Buttercup family, Ranunculaceae.

Notes: An attractive species but with a very short flowering period and if there is no spring rain, may not flower, remaining until the following spring. It is sometimes cultivated in Costa gardens.

RANUNCULUS BULLATUS, **Autumn Buttercup,** Flor de San Diego.

Description: Small perennial dying down in spring; leaves appearing in early autumn, all basal and distinct in having a puffy appearance *(bullate)*, are bright green and glossy with toothed margins. Flower stalks finely hairy, commonly about 20cm tall; flowers solitary about 3.5cm across and so shiny that they appear to have been lacquered.

Flowering: September to December, but from October in the southwest.

Habitat: Abundant in open dry fields often where cattle graze (though it is poisonous to them) and rocky ground in the southwest. Further east it is also abundant amongst limestone rocks, olive groves and open fields from the coast to the hills.

Distribution: Southern Mediterranean, Portugal.

Family: Buttercup family, Ranunculaceae.

Notes: A widespread and lovely species, and a welcome harbinger of the end of hot summer months. Plants grow in such vast colonies that the yellow flowers in the fields look like concentrated sunshine. Most parts of *Ranunculus* are poisonous, yet this species is a very old medicinal herb once used by country people in Spain.

RANUNCULUS FICARIA ssp. FICARIIFORMIS, **Lesser Celandine,**
Celidonia menor.

Description: Perennial leafy herb from about 5-30cm high
with thin tuberous roots mixed with a few fibrous ones. Leaves
hairless and glossy, deep green and long stalked. Flowers few on
erect branched stalks from the base of the plant. "Petals", which
are honey-leaves*, vary in number up to 6-7 and the flower up
to 5cm across; there are only 3 sepals; the achenes which make
up the seed head are softly hairy.

Flowering: December to April, May in mountains.

Habitat: Damp places - ditches and damp grassy fields or in
semi-shade of light woods, abundant.

Distribution: Nearly all of Europe; in southern Spain it
occurs from the coast to high mountains.

Family: Buttercup family, Ranunculaceae.

Notes: Distinguished from other yellow-flowered *Ranunculus* in this
area by having only 3 sepals. As with many *Ranunculus* these plants are
poisonous to animals.

*Honey-leaves differ from ordinary petals by having little pockets near
the base filled with nectar. These attract insects and the pollen from the
stamens brushes off as they probe down.

PAEONIA BROTEROI, **Paeony, Celonia,** Rosa de rejalgar.

Description: Bushy perennial less than a metre tall. Leaves large, hairless, rather blue-green (glaucous), cut into large leaflets, occasionally with lower secondary leaflets. Flowers about 12cm diameter on erect stalks. Carpels softly hairy and filaments (stalks of anthers) yellow.

Flowering: April to June but in higher altitudes June to July.

Habitat: Open and bushy hillsides from about 500m up into the higher mountains from about Gaucin in Malaga province eastwards.

Distribution: Southern Spain and Portugal.

Family: Paeony family, Paeoniaceae.

Notes: A beautiful plant which used to be common around Ronda. Another species, *P. coriacea* grows in similar places in the east and may be confused with the above. It differs by having wider and greener leaflets which are softly hairy underneath and with hairless carpels and red filaments. *P. officinalis* also grows in some of the higher mountains; it has red flowers and leaves cut into narrow leaflets. This widespread species has been used for centuries for medicine. Most parts of Paeonies contain poisonous properties.

***CAPPARIS OVATA*, Caper,** Alcaparra.

Description: Shrub, low growing, usually spiny and with interlaced, almost leafless, branches. Leaves varying in shape but with a small curved spine at the apex and a pair at the base of the stem. Flowers large, more than 5cm across, opening about midday or later.

Flowering: June to October.

Habitat: Rock walls, in crevices, also on dry heavy soil; coast to mountains, sometimes cultivated in coastal sands.

Distribution: Mediterranean region.

Family: Cleome family, Capparidaceae.

Notes: There are two species in Spain and the above description can cover both as they are often seen on roadside cliffs and high banks and used to be common on the coastal banks between Malaga and Almeria. They also grow inland. *C.spinosa*, the other species, is the Caper of commerce, the buds are pickled and are used for *tapas* in eastern Spain; they are also a valuable export item. True C. *spinosa* should have no leaf spine. In the last century they were cultivated in the sandy soil in the neutral ground between Spain and Gibraltar.

***PAPAVER RHOEAS,* Common Red Poppy,** Corn Poppy, Amapola, Ababol.

Description: Hairy annual commonly between 30-60cm tall; stems one to several. Leaves divided into segments, shallow or deeply lobed, the lower stalked; the colour mid-green (not blue-green). Flowers to about 8 or 9cm across, petals with or without a dark basal patch; stems of anthers purple. Capsule hairless and longer than wide.

Flowering: Late March to May, June in higher altitudes.

Habitat: Very common all through our area on roadsides, open places in uncultivated fields or where annual crops are grown.

Distribution: Most of Europe, North Africa; naturalised world-wide.

Family: California Poppy family, Papaveraceae.

Notes: Used in country medicine even though the plant is poisonous and remains so when dry; it is a troublesome weed in cornfields and where cattle graze or eat hay where Poppy has grown.

ALYSSUM SERPYLLIFOLIUM, **Alyssum,** Arenas.

Description: Woody perennial, low growing, variable but often round in shape and up to 60cm high. Leaves small, almost obscured by the heads of flowers, greyish-white beneath. Flower petals each less than 3mm long. Fruit a silicula, dry broadly elliptic, densely covered with fine white hairs each star-shaped, with several rays.

Flowering: June, July.

Habitat: Dry rocky ground and edges of woods on mountain slopes, from about 1,000m to the high mountains (Sierra Nevada).

Distribution: Southern Spain, France, Portugal, North Africa.

Family: Cress family, Cruciferae (Brassicaceae).

Notes: Though often in limestone areas, it also is found on serpentine (Sierra Bermeja near Estepona). There are many mountain species in our area; all with yellow flowers.

***BISCUTELLA FRUTESCENS*,** **Buckler Mustard,** Anteojos.

Description: A bushy and densely branched perennial growing to 50-60cm in height; most parts white hairy. Basal leaves large to 20cm long; upper leaves smaller, variable in shape, stalkless. Flowers in terminal bunches, each petal about 5mm long with a short claw. Seeds in a paired loculus or valve with a hairless rim and slight swellings in the central part.

Flowering: April to July.

Habitat: Steep cliffsides, crevices and in broken rocks on limestone. Hills and mountains usually above 500m.

Distribution: Southern Spain and Balearics, North Africa.

Family: Cress family, Cruciferae (Brassicaceae).

Notes: There are several species in this area which are difficult to separate. The double loculi, typical of this genus, do not split open like pods. The Spanish name refers to the goggle-like appearance of these fruits.

IBERIS CRENATA, **Candytuft,** Carraspique.

Description: Branched annual or biennial from a few centimetres tall to about 30cm. Leaves hairy, narrow with notched (crenate) margins, but uppermost may be entire. Flowers chalk-white in rather flat heads, petals unequal in size. Fruits hairy, erect, each with a pair of dry and pointed wings.

Flowering: Late March in lowlands, to June.

Habitat: Sand, dry rubbly ground, limestone areas, coastal to the hills. In the southwest on edges of coastal cork or pine woods.

Distribution: Endemic to Spain.

Family: Cress family, Cruciferae (Brassicaceae).

Notes: There are many species of *Iberis* in Spain and most are difficult to identify without ripe fruits. One of the most beautiful is the Gibraltar Candytuft, *I. gibraltarica*; it is endemic to that limestone outcrop and flowers from February to early May.

LOBULARIA MARITIMA, **Sea Alyssum, Sweet Alison,** Herba blanca.

Description: Small perennial herb with a thick tuberous root descending deeply; plant densely leafy, flat or with weak ascending flowering stalks to about 40cm. Leaves small, from rather dark green to silvery with silky hairs. Flowers about 5mm across or less, petals separate, rounded, white occasionally flushed with pink; sweet scented (hay). Two seeds in a capsule, one in each envelope (loculus).

Flowering: About October to June, as soon as autumn rains commence.

Habitat: Grazed fields, beaches and other sandy areas, rocky places; often as a weed in gardens. Abundant, coastal to hills.

Distribution: Southern Europe, North Africa.

Family: Cress family, Cruciferae (Brassicaceae).

Notes: When young the flowers appear to be in heads, but are actually born on short stalks on a leafy stem which extends as flowering progresses. This ubiquitous plant is commonly grown in gardens and there are now many cultivars with large and coloured flowers. In the plate, the grey leaves belong to the curry plant.

PISTORINIA HISPANICA, **Spanish Crassula,** Crasula roja, Puntarilla preciosa.

Description: Small fleshy annual with fine hairs. Stems short, erect about 15cm high. Leaves oblong and fleshy with glandular hairs and usually pinkish, about 1cm long. Flowers, about 2cm diameter are starlike, and have a long slender tube of copper-red; calyx short. Plants grow together in small open clusters.

Flowering: Late June to August.

Habitat: Frequent locally in hills and mountains in sandy places amongst limestone rocks, occasionally in lowlands.

Distribution: Spain and North Africa; throughout southern Spain mainly hills and mountains.

Family: Houseleek family, Crassulaceae.

Notes: Although only a tiny plant, the colour of the flowers is so vivid, they are conspicuous especially when several are growing together. There is another species in Southern Spain, *P. breviflora,* which has yellow flowers and dull reddish underneath. The tube is wider, especially near the top. Mainly in low altitudes in sandy soil, frequent in undisturbed pine woods.

SEDUM ACRE, **Stonecrop,** Wall Pepper, Uvas de gato.

Description: Small creeping herb, hairless. Leaves fleshy, 3-6mm, basal dead, white and papery. Flower stems about 5-12cm high, erect; flowers terminal, 5 petals, 10 stamens.

Flowering: May to July.

Habitat: Dry stony places preferring limestone and usually in the hills; rare below 400m.

Distribution: Most of Europe, North Africa; hills and mountains of our area; often cultivated.

Family: Houseleek family, Crassulaceae.

Notes: Most variable in size, leaf shape, height and in flower size. There are other similar species so the important features of Wall Pepper are given above. The peppery leaves may be eaten in small amounts and have some medicinal value, but in excess are probably poisonous.

SEDUM SEDIFORME, **Green Stonecrop,** Uvas de pajaro.

Description: Perennial herb with long woody stems, untidy after flowering; new ones before flowers rather soft and to about 15cm high. Leaves fleshy, grey-green, about 2cm long but less than half a centimetre at the widest part (base) and tapered to a long point. Flowers in terminal heads at the ends of a long stalk commonly about 40 or 50cm, stiffly erect and almost leafless; each flower very small but many on inverted branchlets which are joined together at the base.

Flowering: May or June to July; August in high altitudes.

Habitat: Rough dry ground; crevices in rocks from lowlands to over 3,000m.

Distribution: Mediterranean region, Portugal.

Family: Houseleek family, Crassulaceae.

Notes: A distinct species amongst this large and often difficult genus with its pale green flowers on recurved heads. Attractive when in flower but becomes untidy and ugly later.

***SEDUM TENUIFOLIUM*,** Stonecrop.

Description: Small perennial fleshy herb with erect flowering stems. Leaves usually dead at flowering, lowest long pointed with a widened base and whitish when dead. Flowers in a rather one-sided loose cluster on stems to about 20cm; petals 5-8, often with a reddish central vein; stamens 10 or more.

Flowering: April to July.

Habitat: Dry stony areas and crevices amongst rocks, commonly in hills and mountains.

Distribution: Mediterranean region, Portugal, in southern Spain less common in the Southwest.

Family: Houseleek family, Crassulaceae.

Notes: There are similar yellow-flowered species in the same habitats that may be difficult to separate, but none has the widened basal leaves. *S.forsteranum* has leaves flat on upper surfaces, flowers in a more congested head and petals without the red vein. *S.reflexum* looks similar but leaves are very small, flowerbuds droop and flowers are in a crowded head also without coloured petal veins. None has the one-sided flowerhead.

SAXFRAGA BOISSIERI, **Saxifrage**, Saxifraga.

Description: Perennial in a loose cushion; bulbils present in axils of stem leaves, branches spreading; flowering stems long. Leaves glandular-hairy, 3 leaf lobes deeply divided almost to the base. Flowers 4-7mm across, petals hairless.

Flowering: May to July.

Habitat: Limestone areas in shaded rock crevices, usually damp places in mountains from west of Grazalema and the Sierra de Jarastepa and all through the Serrania de Ronda.

Distribution: Endemic to the mountains behind the Costa del Sol.

Family: Saxifrage family, Saxifragaceae.

Notes: Although restricted in its range it is common there and has been included as it is similar to another species, S. *gemmulosa*, and the two are often confused. In the latter the middle segment of the 3 leaf-lobes is tapered stalk-like to its base; bulbils are at ground level and the plant forms a tighter clump. Also a limestone species of rock crevices, it occurs throughout the mountains of southern Spain.

SAXIFRAGA GLOBULIFERA, **Saxifrage,** Saxifraga.

Description: Perennial herb forming rather loose cushions in rock crevices. Leaves pale green and mainly deeply 3-lobed, glandular hairy. Flowers nearly 1cm wide, calyx hairy; flowering stems reddish 7-12cm long bearing 3-7 flowers.

Flowering: March to June or early July.

Habitat: Usually in crevices, small fissures and overhangs on steep cliff sides, also on mossy rocks in shaded places. Limestone mountains from about Gaucin eastwards, usually above 500m. Also in Gibraltar.

Distribution: Southern Spain, North Africa.

Family: Saxifrage family, Saxifragaceae.

Notes: Could be confused with S. *reuterana* which grows in similar habitats in the mountains around Grazalema and Ronda. It differs in having shorter flowering stems (4-6cm) with 1-2 larger flowers. The Meadow Saxifrage, S. *granulata* of northern and western Europe also grows here from the southwest at about sea-level to the mountains eastwards.

PRUNUS PROSTRATA, Minature Wild Plum.

Description: Flat and spreading deciduous perennial with thick woody and interlacing branches; more or less flat except in sheltered places then growing to about 60cm high; new shoots softly hairy. Leaves often less than 1cm long, margins toothed in the upper part at least; hairless above, grey-hairy below. Flowers about 1-1.5cm across, pale to bright pink. Fruit like a tiny plum, red.

Flowering: June to August.

Habitat: In crevices and on the rocky ground of rock faces, mainly limestone, above 800m to very high altitudes (Sierra Nevada).

Distribution: Mountains of Mediterranean countries (excluding France), North Africa.

Family: Hawthorn and Apple family, Rosaceae

Notes: A small and easily overlooked plant when flowerless, not uncommon in the higher mountains behind the Costa del Sol.

***ROSA SEMPERVIRENS*, Mediterranean White Briar,** Mosqueta común

Description: Evergreen rose, bush forming, or more commonly clambering high into bushes and trees using its thorns on the long stems. Leaflets shiny, in 1-3 pairs with a large terminal one; the basal pair are the smallest. Flowers, white flat and often in small clusters of 3-8; not glandular.

Flowering: From late April to June, but in the hills until early July. It has a short flowering period.

Habitat: In light woods and damp places, very common in the southwest in the lowlands and in hills behind the Costa del Sol.

Distribution: Southern Europe and Morocco.

Family: Hawthorn and Apple family, Rosaceae.

Notes: Common in cork woods but may be confused with another species which flowers from early April, R. *pouzinii*. It is similar but drops its leaves in winter, has glandular hairs on parts of the flower and sepals are lobed (entire in R. *sempervirens*).

***ADENOCARPUS TELONENSIS*, Southern Adenocarpus,**
Racavieja, Rascavieja.

Description: Woody much branched but open shrub about 1.5m high; twigs pale rather rough. Leaves divided into threes, leaflets very small, about 8 x 4mm at most, hairless above, hairy below; clustered on twigs. Flowers in open clusters up to 7 on tops of branchlets, never dense; corolla about 1.5-2cm long, the standard softly hairy above as is the calyx. Pods narrow, covered with swollen yellow glands and some long hairs.

Flowering: April to June.

Habitat: Open scrubland, lowlands and hills, locally common.

Distribution: Southern and central Spain, southern France, Portugal, North Africa.

Family: Sweet Pea family, Leguminosae (Fabaceae).

Notes: There are four species in Spain and they are distinguished from other brooms by their densely glandular and narrow pods. Another species, *A.decorticans* which is common in the mountains of our area, is magnificent when in flower, about April or May. Growing up to 3m it has dense clusters of rich yellow flowers covering the plant; pods are oblong and also glandular.

CALICOTOME VILLOSA, **Spiny Broom,** Érguenes.

Description: Very spiny shrub, 1-2m but commonly smaller; new growth clothed with silvery hairs; spines straight, tough, 3-4cm long; extremely sharp, terminating the short leafy twigs and remaining on dead wood. Leaves divided into three blunt leaflets which are dark blue-green and softly hairy underneath; they fall in summer. Flowers rich yellow, scented, in bunches of 2-15 in such profusion when fully out that they hide the leaves; calyx densely covered with soft hairs. Legume 3-4cm long, densely covered with silvery hairs; margins thickened.

Flowering: March to early May.

Habitat: In open places especially dry hillsides with Genista and Gorse bushes. Flowers nearly all come out together and is then spectacular in its abundance.

Distribution: Mediterranean, southern Spain, southern Portugal.

Family: Sweet Pea family, Leguminosae (Fabaceae).

Notes: A formidable shrub to encounter at close quarters, but beautiful in flower. The spiny branches are so imbricated that a stand of them is almost impenetrable. In the past, goatherds used to cut bushes of these to use as corrals for their goats.

CORONILLA VALENTINA ssp. GLAUCA, **Large Scorpion-Vetch,** Carolina.

Description: Bushy, soft shrub commonly about 1m high. Leaves rather pale blue-green, divided into 2-3 pairs of blunt-ended leaflets with a terminal one. Flowers with corolla 7-12mm long and up to 10 scented flowers in each head. Pods hanging about 3-5cm long, very narrow with constrictions between the seeds.

Flowering: January to March in Gibraltar; February to May in most other places.

Habitat: Rocky and open ground, mainly limestone; from coast to the mountains.

Distribution: Mediterranean Europe, Portugal, North Africa; only the subspecies occuring in our area.

Family: Sweet Pea family, Leguminosae (Fabaceae).

Notes: An attractive shrub common in limestone areas and abundant in Gibraltar in gardens and on the upper rock. The common name refers to the pods which are curved, jointed and with a pointed end like the sting of a scorpion.

CYTISUS BAETICUS, **Southwest Broom,** Escobón negro.

Description: Tall erect shrub 2-4m; twigs with 7 angles. Leaves stalked, 3-foliate, flowers amongst the leaves, 1-3 together, calyx with fine hairs or none, style curved, almost hairless. Legume (seedpod) densely woolly with silvery hairs of uneven length, pod almost straight.

Flowering: January to about April.

Habitat: Moist woods, shady edges of streams and also on rocky slopes of hills in the southwest; often associated with corkwoods.

Distribution: Southwest Spain to hills near Grazalema, Portugal, North Africa.

Family: Sweet Pea family, Leguminosae (Fabaceae).

Notes: One of the earliest Brooms to flower here, they were once much eaten by goats, and then flowered when about a metre tall. There are three similar species in southern Spain that are most difficult to separate and some differences are given under *C.grandiflorus* (p.56).

CYTISUS GRANDIFLORUS, **Broom,** Escobón.

Description: Tall shrub to about 3m; twigs 5 angled. Leaves small, stalkless and mainly 1-foliate (undivided). Flowers solitary or in pairs, calyx hairless; style in an open coil, the lower part hairy. Legume compressed, straight, densely clothed in long white hairs. Pod turns black when mature.

Flowering: April to July.

Habitat: Bushy and shaded rocky places, usually damp; also streamsides in tall woods in the mountains. Not common in the southwest.

Distribution: Southern Spain, Portugal, North Africa.

Family: Sweet Pea family, Leguminosae (Fabaceae).

Notes: There are 3 similar species in southern Spain of about the same height, flowering about the same time. Some main differences are: C. BAETICUS: Twigs 7-8 angled. Leaves stalked. Flowers 1-3; calyx almost hairless. Legume flat. C. STRIATUS *(Escobón negro)*: Twigs 8-10 angled. Leaves stalkless. Flowers 1-2 (occasionally 3); calyx densely hairy, style coiled, hairy. Legume slightly inflated. C. GRANDIFLORUS: Twigs 5 angled. Leaves stalkless. Flowers 1-2; calyx hairless. Legume strongly compressed.

ERINACEA ANTHYLLIS, **Blue Hedgehog Broom,** Abrojo, Piorno azul.

Description: Spiny and dense low-growing shrub to about 1m in height. Leaves on the stout spines small, to 2cm long, simple or divided into three, dark green. Flowers blue-violet, about 1cm long with a swollen calyx; pods to 2cm long, hairy.

Flowering: May to early August.

Habitat: Rocky and exposed mountain slopes to alpine rocks, from about 1,000m (Sierra Bermeja and Grazalema amongst Pinsapo Firs), mainly limestone.

Distribution: Southern and eastern Spain, France, North Africa.

Family: Sweet Pea family, Leguminosae (Fabaceae).

Notes: A most distinctive legume when in flower. A high mountain plant amongst what is termed the Hedgehog Zone where most plants are reduced in size, and are dense and spiny for protection.

***GALEGA OFFICINALIS,* Goat's Rue,** Ruda cabruna.

Description: Erect perennial herb, commonly about 1.5m high; soft, hardly woody. Leaves divided into 4-10 large leaflets with a terminal one. Flowers few to many in erect racemes; buds greenish-white, flowers from pale lilac to blue-lilac. Pods almost erect, long and narrow, pointed, about 2-6cm X 3-4mm.

Flowering: April to May.

Habitat: Open damp meadows, low-lying grassy ground near streams; lowlands to mountains; occasionally cultivated in our area for fodder.

Distribution: Most of Europe, cultivated elsewhere; North Africa.

Family: Sweet Pea family, Leguminosae (Fabaceae).

Notes: Should not be confused with *Vicia cracca,* a weak climbing annual with small leaflets to 15 pairs and a 3-pronged tendril at the apex; flowers are lilac to blue-lilac in erect heads.

***GENISTA CINEREA*, Slender Broom,** Ginesta pequeña, Retama macho.

Description: Slender spineless shrub of about 1.5m with soft pale hairs on branches, leaves and the calyx. Branches long and spreading. Leaves small, not more than 1cm long. Flowers rich yellow in sessile pairs; the standard has a ridge of soft hairs on the back (see Notes).

Flowering: April to July.

Habitat: Rocky limestone hills, open countryside in dry places from low altitudes to mountains but not in extreme southwest.

Distribution: Southwest Mediterranean, Portugal; North Africa.

Family: Sweet Pea family, Leguminosae (Fabaceae).

Notes: A graceful and attractive *Genista*; it covers hillsides with yellow, especially around Ronda and behind the Costa del Sol in late spring. A similar species grows in the east of our area. It differs mainly by having more flowers together, and that the standard is almost all hairy, *(G.ramosissima)* but these and other brooms are very difficult to separate into species.

GENISTA HIRSUTA, **Needle Furze,** Aulaga.

Description: Spiny, small and compact shrub, 30-100cm high typically round on top. Leaves simple, small about 1cm long, margins and lower surface with sparse long hairs. Flowers in a terminal raceme. Standard petal is pointed and usually hairless; small bracteoles are at the top of a flower stalk, together with larger leaf-like bracts. Legume small, about 5mm long and softly hairy; there is one seed.

Flowering: Early April to July.

Habitat: Heavy or gravelly soil, usually in open places and amongst other small shrubs; amongst rocks on high hillsides; in dryish soil (sandy soil in the southwest) but more frequent from about Estepona eastwards; coastal to at least 1,000m.

Distribution: Spain, Portugal, North Africa.

Family: Sweet Pea family, Leguminosae (Fabaceae).

Notes: Could be confused with *G.tournefortii* which has branched spines and bracts at the base of the flower stalk. The standard is notched (emarginate) and softly hairy all over.

GENISTA (TELINE) LINIFOLIA, **Southern Whin,** Escobón blanca.

Description: Woody shrub to about 2m in height. Leaves nearly all stalkless, long, narrow and finely hairy on both surfaces and close-pressed; margins slightly rolled under. Flowers in terminal and usually rather compressed heads, produced in great abundance; flowers with honey scent. Pods short, pointed, lightly covered with pale, soft hairs.

Flowering: March to May or June in hills.

Habitat: Bushy slopes especially near the sea; light woods, very common in the west in the lowlands; up to medium heights in the hills.

Distribution: Western Mediterranean area, Spain (including the Balearics), France.

Family: Sweet Pea family, Leguminosae (Fabaceae).

Notes: Formerly *Teline linifolia.* Often absent from wide areas in southern Spain, and where another species, *G.monspellanus* occurs. They rarely mix, but if so tend to hybridise.

***GENISTA TRIDENS,* Western Whin,** Giniesta, Aulaga.

Description: Small spiny shrub growing to 80cm, with imbricated branches. Leaves small, less than 1cm long, most are divided into 3 leaflets, but some undivided; stipules at the base of the leaves, spiny. Flowers crowded towards the branch ends, honey scented. Pods small nearly 1cm long and hairless.

Flowering: Variable, usually from April to June, but some years flowering in November and December.

Habitat: Heathlands and open rocky ground mainly in leached acid or neutral soils of the west and southwest in our area.

Distribution: Southern Spain to about Grazalema, North Africa.

Family: Sweet Pea family, Leguminosae (Fabaceae)

Notes: Very similar and difficult to distinguish from another species, *G.triacanthos,* which tends to have the flowers spread along the twigs; stipules at the base of a leaf not spiny, and pods are covered with silky hairs. It usually flowers earlier, from March, but there seems little else that is botanically different. Scattered flowers may remain on the plant during autumn and early winter.

HEDYSARUM CORONARIUM, **Crown-vetch,** Crown Sanfoin, Sulla.

Description: Perennial herb with weak leafy stems to about 1m long, but spreading and usually not much higher than 20cm. Leaves divided into about five pairs of dull green leaflets, softly hairy and blunt. Flowers in heads. Seedpods constricted between the seeds, hairless.

Flowering: March to June.

Habitat: Open countryside and road edges; often covering the ground in great masses, especially in sloping grassy fields.

Distribution: West Mediterranean area, often naturalised and cultivated in France, Greece and Portugal. Low altitudes.

Family: Sweet Pea family, Leguminosae (Fabaceae).

Notes: Sometimes called French Honeysuckle, but is not related. Commonly cultivated for fodder. Could be confused with *Hedysarum glomeratum,* an annual with paler flowers, smaller heads.

LATHYRUS TINGITANUS, **Southern Vetchling,** Alverjana de tanger.

Description: Annual, hairless and long-climbing with winged stems growing to a metre or more; blue-green. Leaves in pairs, each about 3-8cm long, varying from narrow to almost oval. Flowers 1-3, each about 2.5-4cm on a long stalk; calyx shorter than its tube with teeth of equal length. Pods variable about 7-8cm long, hairless and beaked.

Flowering: April to June, July in hills.

Habitat: Seasonally damp and low-lying ground, fields and uncultivated places, edges of woods by streams, climbing over shrubs in lowlands to mid mountains.

Distribution: Southern Spain, Portugal, Sardinia, Africa.

Family: Sweet Pea family, Leguminosae (Fabaceae).

Notes: Could be confused with the garden Sweet Pea *(L.odoratus)* which sometimes becomes naturalised along the coast, but Southern Vetchling is scentless. The Latin name *tingitanus* suggests it was native to Tangier (Tingis, the classical city of great antiquity).

LOTUS CRETICUS, **Sand Lotus,** Bird's foot-Trefoil, Trebol de cuernos.

Description: Perennial with almost woody base, low growing and spreading. Leaves divided into 5 leaflets covered with soft silvery hairs. Flowers 2-6 in loose heads, keel with a purple tip. Seed-pods very narrow, about 3-4cm X 2-3mm, almost straight and several spreading from a central point.

Flowering: March to May.

Habitat: Sand dunes and sandy shores, coastal.

Distribution: Mediterranean region, Portugal, North Africa.

Family: Sweet Pea family, Leguminosae (Fabaceae).

Notes: There are many *Lotus* species in Southern Spain and most are rather difficult to separate, but the densely silver leaves and habitat make this one easier, except perhaps for *L.arenarius* which also grows in coastal sands but is a slender annual.

LUPINUS MICRANTHUS, **Hairy Blue Lupin,** Altramuz.

Description: Annual less than 40cm high, softly hairy, hairs silvery or brown. Leaves dull green, leaflets usually widest towards the tips. Flowers in a comparatively close head; standard with white in the centre; keel with a dark tip.

Flowering: April to June.

Habitat: Sandy soil in grassy fields, road verges, coastal to mid mountains in acid soils.

Distribution: Mediterranean area, Portugal, North Africa, either native or naturalised; frequently cultivated.

Family: Sweet Pea family, Leguminosae (Fabaceae).

Notes: Most Lupins dislike lime and many are poisonous especially to stock, but there is one species *(L.albus)* with edible dried seeds (poisonous when fresh) which is cultivated in our area mainly in the sandy soils of the southwest. It has rather dreary whitish flowers. Another species which is common *(L.angustifolius)* has blue flowers and very narrow leaflets. The very common yellow-flowered Lupin is *L.luteus.*

ONONIS NATRIX, **Yellow Restharrow,** Beluda, Pegamoscas.

Description: Shrub, small and much branched, from about 20cm to less than a metre high; most parts sticky with glandular hairs. Leaves mainly 3-foliate, leaflets variable in shape, toothed margins. Flowers up to 2cm long and frequently with a few fine red veins. Pods hairy, up to 2.5cm long.

Flowering: April to July.

Habitat: Dry sandy or rocky ground, uncultivated places, country roadsides; coastal to hills and some mountains.

Distribution: South and west Europe, North Africa.

Family: Sweet Pea family, Leguminosae (Fabaceae).

Notes: There are many yellow-flowered species in our area and almost as many with pink flowers. *O. natrix* has three sub-species which vary slightly from each other and occur in southern Spain.

***ONONIS SPECIOSA*, Lupin-headed Restharrow,** Rascavieja, Garbancillo.

Description: Woody shrub about 2m tall with sticky glandular hairs. Leaves divided into 3 large leaflets. Flowers in long dense heads, each flower about 1.5-2cm long, varying from pale to rich yellow. Pods very small, almost oval, hairy.

Flowering: May to July.

Habitat: Rocky places amongst other shrubs, mountain slopes in rubble or in rock crevices; usually above 300m but absent from some areas.

Distribution: Southern Spain, North Africa.

Family: Sweet Pea family, Leguminosae (Fabaceae).

Notes: A conspicuous shrub when the erect heads are in flower; locally common.

RETAMA SPHAEROCARPA, **Yellow Retama,** Retama.

Description: Shrub to 3m, sparsely leafy and with thin whippy pale yellow-green branches. Leaves small narrow, deciduous, covered with pale and very fine silky hairs. Flowers small, to about 8mm long, standard almost round. Pod 7-9mm, round, smooth; 1-2 seeds.

Flowering: May to July.

Habitat: Dry banks, open countryside, locally very common from Jimena eastwards; from about 300m to the mountains.

Distribution: Spain, Portugal, North Africa.

Family: Sweet Pea family, Leguminosae (Fabaceae).

Notes: Referred to in some books as *Lygos sphaerocarpa.* Conspicuous shrub when in flower in open ground bordering country roadsides; they have a curious cloying scent. When flowerless the finely ribbed branches get a whitish sheen on them. There is another species, *R. monosperma*, growing in southwest coastal sands and inland to about Jerez. It has heavily scented white flowers and a one-seeded, rather rough pod with a terminal curved point (mucro).

TETRAGONOLOBUS PURPUREA, Asparagus Pea.

Description: Annual, low growing, softly hairy. Leaves divided into 3 leaflets, the middle usually largest. Flowers solitary or in pairs. Pods about 4-5 X 0.8cm with 4 wavy wings of the same colour.

Flowering: March to April.

Habitat: Seasonally damp and open meadows, cultivated fields, roadside banks; coastal to hills.

Distribution: Southern Europe (not Portugal), North Africa; also cultivated (for its edible pods).

Family: Sweet Pea family, Leguminosae (Fabaceae).

Notes: Distinctive because of its flower colour and winged pod which has a delicate flavour but needs to be used when very young as it becomes woody with maturity. Another species in our area is *T. conjugatus*, also with red flowers, but long thin pods without the wavy wings.

ULEX PARVIFLORUS, **Gorse,** Furze, Aulaga morena.

Description: Spiny shrub, variable in size, shape and length of branches; shoots usually softly hairy; phyllodes green spine-like replacing normal leaves and about 0.5cm long; spines green to about 3cm long, straight or curved.   Flowers with a yellowish, slightly hairy calyx divided into two, one with 2 teeth, the other with 3 at the apex.

Flowering: December to April, but in some sub-species from March to May.

Habitat: Open heathlands and rocky hill slopes; coastal to high mountains.

Distribution: Southwest Europe.

Family: Sweet Pea family, Leguminosae (Fabaceae).

Notes: There are several sub-species in our area, often difficult to separate. Perhaps the most attractive is the one in the plate, ssp. *parviflorus* which is common throughout. In the sun, the strong honey scent attracts many butterflies.

OXALIS PES-CAPRAE, **Bermuda Buttercup,** Vinagrera.

Description: Small soft plant without a main stem and with bulbs deeply buried in the ground. Leaves pale and hairless divided into 3 leaflets on a long main stalk usually about 15cm long in open places but can be over 25cm if in semi-shade. Flowers about 3cm across, several together on stalks from a central point; clear lemon-yellow without any variation, except in a rather rare double form which is paler.

Flowering: December to early May, later in hills.

Habitat: Nearly everywhere, mainly open places but a pest in gardens; covering fields and roadsides in vast patches.

Distribution: Native of South Africa, naturalised in most Mediterranean countries and in Portugal, Florida, Bermuda, increasing its range. In our area in any soil from the coast to limestone crevices at least to 500m.

Family: Wood-sorrel family, Oxalidaceae.

Notes: Though most attractive when covering fields with yellow during early spring and being a foodplant of the lovely Cleopatra butterfly, it is a serious pest, covering many hectares of valuable agricultural land. The plants contain oxalic acid and are not eaten by domestic animals. Not related to buttercups *(Ranunculus).*

ERODIUM PRIMULACEUM, **Andaluz Storksbill,** Aguja de pastor.

Description: Small annual to about 30cm, usually smaller with several weak and sprawling thin stems, slightly aromatic. Leaves deeply cut to the midrib (pinnate) or nearly so (pinnatifid), margins toothed. Flowers on long thin stalks about 2-6 together in an open and stalked head; each flower about 2-2.5cm across with two petals larger than others and with a dark pink mark near the base on each. Flower colour pale to mid-pink, occasionally white.

Flowering: December to May.

Habitat: Sands, gravel and grassy fields; amongst scrub and in light woods; common in lowlands to hills.

Distribution: Southern Spain, Portugal, North Africa.

Family: Storksbill family, Geraniaceae.

Notes: In early spring it becomes conspicuous with large patches of pink on roadsides and fields. Often included as a sub-species of *G. cicutarium* the Common Cranesbill, which has a wide range throughout Europe; it is more robust and the evenly sized petals are without a dark mark.

GERANIUM MALVIFLORUM, **Ronda Cranesbill,** Guellas de Ronda.

Description: Soft perennial herb with erect flowering stalks about 30cm high; hairs pale, not sticky. Leaves deeply cut into narrow lobes, these cut again into segments. Flowers large, about 3-5cm across, blue-lilac to pinkish.

Flowering: May to early July.

Habitat: Usually above 650m, rough or rocky ground, seasonally damp meadows, in scrub or light woods especially under deciduous shrubs (Hawthorn, *Acer* etc.).

Distribution: Southern Spain, North Africa. In our area from the mountains near Grazalema to Jaen province.

Family: Storksbill family, Geraniaceae.

Notes: An attractive species which is common in the mountain meadows behind the Costa del Sol. It somewhat resembles a slender Meadow Cranesbill, but with lilac flowers and even more deeply cut leaves. The latter is rare in the south.

LINUM NARBONENSE, **Large Blue Flax, Beautiful Flax,** Lino bravo.

Description: Glabrous perennial, slender and spreading to 50cm high or more. Leaves narrow with 1-3 parallel veins, blue-green. Flowers vivid Gentian-blue to 3.5cm across; sepals with thin papery margins.

Flowering: April to July.

Habitat: Amongst rocks and gravelly places; on open hillsides from about 300m to mountains.

Distribution: West and central Mediterranean area, Portugal, North Africa.

Family: Linen flax family, Linaceae.

Notes: Easily distinguished from other blue-flowered flax species in our area which have either pale or smaller flowers. There are also about 5 species with yellow flowers. The cultivated flax, L. *usitatissimum* is grown here and has become naturalised; flowers are bright blue but less than 2cm across.

LINUM SUFFRUTICOSUM, **White Flax,** Hierba sanjuana, Lino blanco.

Description: Small, much-branched perennial herb to about 50cm high and wide. Leaves dark green, short, very narrow, about 1mm wide with rough margins, which are rolled under. Flowers about 3cm wide, have very pale yellow buds but open white, usually with a crimson claw at the base of the petal, or stamens and styles are red, showing a dark centre.

Flowering: From late April to June or July.

Habitat: Usually common from above 800m, in rock crevices, on rubble and dry places on roadsides.

Distribution: Spain, France, Italy, North Africa. In southern Spain it is a conspicuous plant from about Ronda eastwards.

Family: Linen Flax family, Linaceae.

Notes: Several sub-species of the White Flax are recognised and the Spanish form may be one of these. The annual blue flaxes of colder climates also grow in southern Spain, as well as a small yellow-flowered annual (L.*strictum*).

EUPHORBIA NICAEENSIS, **Southern Spurge,** Lechetrezna.

Description: Perennial, often nearly a metre tall; erect pinkish stems. Leaves sea-green (glaucous). Flowers yellowish, without petals; in stalked heads, each flower surrounded by yellow rays and bracteoles; male flower with a single stamen, female more or less round surrounded by the male; glands usually with two small horns. Capsule wrinkled about 4mm; seeds ovoid, nearly smooth, pale grey.

Flowering: May to July.

Habitat: Open places, roadside banks and amongst low shrubs, lowlands to hills.

Distribution: Much of Europe, North Africa.

Family: Dog's Mercury family, Euphorbiaceae.

Notes: There are many Euphorbias in our area, most being difficult to separate. Ripe seeds are necessary for identification; they vary in size and colour, if their capsules are smooth or rough and if the little glands are horned or not.

POLYGALA MICROPHYLLA, **Spanish Milkwort**, Poligala.

Description: Woody herb or very small shrub with thin but tough stems, 15-30cm high. Leaves hairless, small and narrow, pointed, usually falling prior to flowering. Flowers in stalked bunches (racemes) up to 8 and varying from a deep blue to purplish, occasionally purple-pink; corolla nearly 1cm long, sepals 5, the 2 inner (the wings) much larger than the 3 outer; petals 3, the lower (keel) different in shape from the others but not crested, as other species are. Capsule compressed but almost round in shape, less than 1cm long by half wide.

Flowering: February to June.

Habitat: Dry places amongst heathers and other shrubs, open woods, often in sandy soil in rock crevices.

Distribution: Southern Spain, Portugal; in our area from about 250m to over 850m.

Family: Polygala family, Polygalaceae.

Notes: Conspicuous when in flower. There are several species in southern Spain, some have paler flowers and others with a crest or fringe on the keel; a similar species is P.*baetica* with a crest and is endemic to western Spain.

PISTACIA LENTISCUS, **Lentisc, Mastic,** Lentisco, Almaciga.

Description: Aromatic spreading shrub to small tree, from about 1m to at least 6m in height, trunk rather dark. Leaves divided into leaflets commonly with 3-4 pairs occasionally a few more; midrib (rachis) with a flat narrow wing on either side, usually extending just beyond the last pair. Flowers in tight clusters, no petals; male and female in separate flowers and on different plants (dioecious), the male with yellow stamens and wind pollinated; the female with style and ovary and usually light red. Fruit, a drupe, is round, about half a centimeter across with a tiny pointed tip, shiny and green at first ripening red then black; very strong smelling.

Flowering: April to June; fruits usually not ripening until October or November.

Habitat: In open uncultivated or grazed country, rough and dry ground, or heathlands forming low scrub and rocky areas in higher altitudes; very common from the coast to the hills.

Distribution: Mediterranean area, Portugal.

Family: Mango family, Anacardiaceae.

Notes: A useful plant known to the ancient world. The bark produces mastic gum or resin and all parts are strongly but unpleasantly aromatic.

***PISTACIA TEREBINTHUS*, Terebinth, Turpentine Tree,** Terebinto.

Description: Aromatic woody shrub or small tree to about 5m but usually smaller; deciduous. Leaves divided into a few large leaflets and one terminal; midrib unwinged. Flowers dioecious (see Lentisc p.79) small in open clusters (panicles); no petals, stamens 3-5, creamy yellow to brownish. Fruit green at first, then red, eventually turning brown.

Flowering: April to June.

Habitat: Mainly amongst limestone rocks, in crevices, commonly on mountain slopes, and in open places and amongst short scrub.

Distribution: Mediterranean region, Portugal, North Africa; in dry places.

Family: Mango family, Anacardiaceae.

Notes: The plant produces essence of turpentine which has been used for many centuries. Another species, P.*vera*, produces the Pistachio nut; the tree is occasionally cultivated in southern Spain.

LAVATERA MARITIMA, **Sea Mallow,** Malvavisco marino.

Description: A much branched, grey, woody shrub about, or just over a metre in height, often smaller on exposed rocks; new twigs covered with minute grey star-shaped hairs. Leaves with stiff grey hairs, almost round with variously lobed margins and about 4-7cm wide. Flowers about 6cm across; very pale pink but with a deep pink base to the petals which, being narrow, show the green sepals beneath. The three epicalyx segments (see *Malope malacoides* p.82) are almost united at the base and together with the calyx are short and pointed.

Flowering: February to April.

Habitat: Nearly always by the sea on rocky cliffs and banks and in rubbly dry ground, open places.

Distribution: Mediterranean; mainly Spain, France and Italy; North Africa. In southern Spain it is an eastern species and very common in Almeria province.

Family: Hollyhock and Hibiscus family, Malvaceae.

Notes: The felty grey hairs covering the stems and leaves protect the plant from excessive dehydration from salt-laden winds. In France, the plant used to grow on high limestone cliffs well away from the coast. It also grew as far west as Gibraltar, which is also limestone.

MALOPE MALACOIDES, Malope

Description: Hispid perennial not much higher than 50cm. Leaves about 5cm long have crenate margins and are shallowly lobed or not. Flowers large, each petal about 4-5cm long. Calyx segments free from each other, sharp-pointed and the epicalyx segments (below the calyx) are also free but rounded and shorter. Inside these are many tiny fruits forming a rounded head.

Flowering: April to June.

Habitat: Usually sheltered by low bushes, on roadsides, grazed fields in sandy or rubbly gound, open places.

Distribution: Southern Europe, North Africa. Common locally in southern Spain.

Family: Hollyhock and Hibiscus family, Malvaceae.

Notes: The epicalyx is a calyx-like bract and subtends the usually different shaped calyx. It is present in many of this vast family which includes the garden Hibiscus, also Cotton which is an important economic crop in southern Spain, ripening in late summer.

MALVA SYLVESTRIS, **Common Mallow,** Malva común.

Description: Woody herb about 1m high or more, variable in habit but usually biennial; much branched and woody at the base. Leaves with simple and star-shaped hairs, 3-7 round or pointed lobes, shallow to deep. Flowers 4-6cm across, calyx with small star-shaped hairs, epicalyx (see *Malope malacoides* p.) 2-3 and shorter than the calyx.

Flowering: February to July.

Habitat: In open areas, edges of woods, in roadside rubble; very common, especially in alkaline soils.

Distribution: Widely distributed in Europe, North Africa; in southern Spain coastal to the hills.

Family: Hollyhock and Hibiscus family, Malvaceae.

Notes: Most of the *Malva* and other close genera in this area may be difficult to name and some hybridise. All *Malva* have an epicalyx of three free lobes below the normal calyx. The leaves of the common Mallow contain a mucilage which has been used in medicine since the birth of Christianity at least.

DAPHNE GNIDIUM, **Mediterranean Daphne,** Torvisco.

Description: Small pale green shrub about 75-150cm high with brown and downy branches more or less erect. Leaves hairless, narrow and between 2-6cm long. Flowers small cream and scented with a tube downy on the outside. Fruit a drupe, scarlet-red.

Flowering: July to October.

Habitat: Coastal sands, uncultivated fields, amongst light growth of other shrubs and open woods, dry soil.

Distribution: Mainly west Mediterranean area, Portugal; in southern Spain from coast to mid mountains, common.

Family: Spurge laurel family, Thymelaeaceae.

Notes: The strange sounding name *gnidium* comes from the Latin *gnidia*, from a town in ancient Turkey. All parts are very poisonous, yet it has been known medicinally for many centuries as a purgative appearing in Materia Medica of Dioscorides, (Greek physician, 2nd century A.D.). In Greek mythology, Daphne, the daughter of Peneus, was changed into a tree, the Bay Laurel, not a Daphne.

DAPHNE LAUREOLA.ssp. LATIFOLIA, **Spurge Laurel,** Adelfilla, Hoja de San Pedro.

Description: Hairless shrub 50-75cm high. Leaves rather fleshy and shiny above, variable in size commonly about 8-15cm long, wider towards the apex. Flowers pale green, faintly scented; fruit a drupe, black and shiny.

Flowering: February to May, June in higher altitudes.

Habitat: From about 400m. In southwest hills, under tall woods of cork and deciduous oaks and Rhododendrons, commonly near streams. Further east under *Abies pinsapo* and other forest trees in the mountains.

Distribution: Most of Europe (not Portugal), North Africa; in southern Spain locally common.

Family: Spurge laurel family, Thymelaeaceae.

Notes: An extremely poisonous plant, leaves, bark and fruit. Animals seem to avoid it possibly because the leaves have an acrid taste.

CISTUS ALBIDUS, **Grey-leaved Sunrose,** Estepa.

Description: An attractive bushy shrub growing to about 2m high, often less. Leaves grey, softly hairy, about 4-6cm long; flowers in varying shades of pink, about 6 to 7cm in diameter; petals crumpled, sepals 5.

Flowering: From February to early July.

Habitat: Not a fussy plant. In sandy soils in coastal pinewoods or in open uncultivated places in rocky hillsides and in limestone. In the mountains it often grows in large masses.

Distribution: Abundant from the east to west in southern Spain, lowlands to mountains. Also in Portugal and west Mediterranean countries to Italy.

Family: Rockrose and Sunrose family, Cistaceae.

Notes: A beautiful bush even without flowers. Tends to hybridise with the small C. *crispus*, with darker pink flowers. A white form is found in stands in some areas, and shows up the grey leaves most beautifully.

CISTUS CRISPUS, **Small pink Cistus,** Jaguarzo prieto, Carpazo.

Description: Woody herb, almost flat or small leafy shrub about 50cm high or less. Leaves about 3-4cm long mainly grey-green with wavy margins, almost blunt; upper leaves near the flowers often narrower and sharper; most parts softly hairy. Flowers 3-6cm across, sepals 5; flower colour from rose-pink to deep purplish-pink.

Flowering: April to June.

Habitat: Bushy and rocky uncultivated ground, also along country paths and roadsides in leached soil and gravel; coastal to hills.

Distribution: Western Mediterranean, Portugal, North Africa.

Family: Rockrose and Sunrose family, Cistaceae.

Notes: Variable in size and shape; in poor soil it may grow into a flat rosette and then is covered with smaller flowers of intense colour.

***CISTUS LADANIFER*, Gum Cistus,** Jara pringosa.

Description:　Large woody shrubs; leaves narrow, about 6-10cm long, dark green and very sticky above, greyish underneath. Flowers pure white (see Notes below) solitary on twiglets, petals crumpled and falling each afternoon, new ones opening early each morning. Sepals 3, greenish; seed capsules very hard and almost round.

Flowering:　March to early June, occasionally to early July.

Habitat:　Leached, sandy and neutral soils, disliking limestone. Rocky open hillsides where it may cover large areas and when in flower looks as though snowflakes have fallen.

Distribution:　Portugal, Spain and southern France. The unblotched form is abundant in southern Spain, especially from the west to about Estepona, and further east where there is no limestone.

Family:　Rockrose and Sunrose family, Cistaceae.

Notes:　A spotted form occurs further north, nearer Seville. The sticky leaves give off a pleasant aromatic scent when the sun is hot. The gum was used as an elixer and later for medicine (*laudanum*). C.*laurifolia*, which looks similar, has flowers in clusters at the twig ends; leaves are grey-green and dull and it occurs mainly in the mountains further east.

CISTUS SALVIFOLIUS, **White Cistus,** Jara estepa, Jaguarzo.

Description: A small, much-branched leafy shrub. Twigs, buds and fruits bronze-pink. Grows to about one metre, but flowers when small. Leaves 3-5cm long, widest at the base and with a short stalk. Surface wrinkled and rather dark green, paler below. Petals white, yellow at their bases, about 5cm diameter. Sepals 5 (2 large and 3 small). Seeds very small in hard capsules covered at first by the two, now enlarged, sepals.

Flowering: From late February until at least June, then it becomes covered with bronze-red seed capsules.

Habitat: Not fussy over soils but preferring open places from the coast to hills, in sandy or rocky places and also in cleared or deserted fields.

Distribution: Widespread throughout southern Europe and the Mediterranean. Very common in southern Spain.

Family: Rockrose and Sunrose family, Cistaceae.

Notes: In the spring the bushes become covered with their briar-like white flowers and, although scentless, attract butterflies.

HALIMUM HALIMIFOLIUM, **Yellow Sunrose,** Monte blanco, Juagarzo.

Description: A much branched, woody shrub varying greatly in size and appearance, up to one metre or, when in poor soils, may be low and spreading, flowering when about 30cm high. Leaves small and silvery, hairless but covered with minute scales. Flowers large about 5cm diameter, petals yellow with or without blotches near petal bases. There are 5 sepals covered with silvery scales (not hairs). Dark blotches vary in size from small, to large as in the plate above.

Flowering: From late February to summer

Habitat: In open places on leached soils, especially sandstone (southwest) and in sandy woods of Stone and Aleppo pine. Lowlands and rocky hills mainly coastal.

Distribution: Southern Spain, Portugal and western Mediterranean to Italy.

Family: Rockrose and Sunrose family, Cistaceae.

Notes: A beautiful plant in flower and attractive even in leaf. Petals last only part of a day, and tend to fall as soon as picked. Plants with plain yellow petals appear to come out earlier than the blotched forms.

***HELIANTHEMUM APPENNINUM*,** **Common White Rockrose.**

Description: Small shrubby perennial laxly branched and spreading, usually less than 45cm high. Leaves narrow and about 2.5 long, usually grey-green with tiny star-shaped hairs. Flowers about 2.5cm diameter, the narrow base of the petal (claw) is yellow. Capsules scarcely longer than the accompanying sepals.

Flowering: May to July.

Habitat: Open rocky ground mainly in high hills and mountains of our area, but not in extreme southwest; common.

Distribution: Southern and western Europe, including Britain (southwest England).

Family: Rockrose and Sunrose family, Cistaceae.

Notes: A most variable plant and often not easily distinguished from other species occuring in southern Spain; sometimes leaves are green on the upper side and occasionally flowers are pink.

FRANKENIA LAEVIS, **Sea Heath,** Hierba sapera.

Description: Small mat-forming perennial, mainly flat but sometimes growing to 50cm high if amongst other growth. Leaves very small, heath-like with inrolled margins, blue-green, hairy below or covered with a white crust. Flowers about 1cm wide, whitish to mid or dark pink; solitary and in flat clusters (not in conspicuous spikes).

Flowering: Most of the year, but best in early spring to summer.

Habitat: Saline areas, coastal sands and salt-marshes; in shingle or in mud and gravel, damp grassy places, edges of beaches; also inland around salty edges of shallow lakes.

Distribution: Western Europe to southern England; coastal. Common in southern Spain.

Family: Frankenia family, Frankeniaceae.

Notes: A salt-loving plant. There are 5 species in Spain, 3 of which are endemic to the Iberian Peninsula. Shore birds probably help to distribute the plant to our inland lakes, one near Jerez (Lake Medina) and another near Antequera (Fuente de Piedra) where Sea Heath is common.

***ECBALLIUM ELATERIUM*, Squirting Cucumber,** Cohombrillo amargo.

Description: Low growing perennial with a large and tuberous root; nearly all parts covered with short stiff hairs. Leaves on long stalks. Flowers small, to 2cm across, creamy yellow; male (with only stamens) and female (with a stigma) in separate flowers but on the same plant. The female produces the fruit which is small, about 5cm long, green and rough hairy. It hangs down from the erect stem.

Flowering: From about April until October or November.

Habitat: Prefers basic soils; rubble and gravelly areas on roadsides and waste places, amongst rocks but always in the open.

Distribution: Most Mediterranean countries, Portugal and frequent in southern Spain.

Family: Cucumber and Melon family, Curcubitaceae.

Notes: If touched when ripe the fruit explodes from the base, which is uppermost on the stem. The seeds and juice are ejected with force. Should this get on one's skin it is painful, stinging for a long time. Most parts of the plant, especially the fruit, contain an irritant poison but despite this the plant is used in medicine. Though a close relation of the cucumber, it has no tendrils.

LYTHRUM JUNCEUM, **Rush Loosestrife,** Arroyuelo.

Description: Soft perennial often flowering in the first year. Leaves hairless on non-flowering and nearly flat stems about 10 x 5mm; those on almost erect flowering stems narrower, about 10 x 2mm and erect; stems angled, pale brown. Flowers pink, solitary by a leaf; the green "false calyx" (hypanthium) has a row or two of small, dark-red, squarish dots near its base.

Flowering: April to July.

Habitat: Damp to wet grassy places, ditches by roadsides, above streams in open fields and in light woods, but always near water.

Distribution: Southern Europe, Mediterranean region, North Africa; common in southern Spain.

Family: Loosestrife family, Lythraceae.

Notes: It is a very good butterfly plant worth cultivating for that. The specific name probably refers to the fact that it grows with rushes. There are two other similar species in the same habitat that could be confused with L.*junceum*, but neither has the red dots.

LYTHRUM SALICARIA, **Purple Loosestrife,** Salicaria.

Description: Erect, branched perennial herb up to 1.5m, most parts with short pale hairs; stems leafy, square. Leaves dull, stalkless and widest at the base, apex pointed. Flowers scentless and at first in a single erect spike becoming branched with many (9-10) flowering branchlets; flowers variable in colour 1-1.5cm to 2cm in diameter, from pink to deep lilac-pink; petals narrow, pointed and separate; stamens 10 or more of uneven lengths.

Flowering: June to September.

Habitat: Stream and river banks, marshes in open land or in semi-shade of woods, but always in wet ground.

Distribution: Most of Europe, North Africa; in southern Spain, throughout.

Family: Loosestrife family, Lythraceae.

Notes: In the hot dry weather when little else is in flower, it is conspicuous. Could possibly be mistaken for the Great Willow herb (*Epilobium hirsutum*), which flowers about the same time and until October. The pink flowers are larger and not in a spike, the petals wide and stamens short.

MYRTUS COMMUNIS, **Myrtle,** Mirto común.

Description: Shrub, woody and much branched, commonly about 2-4m tall, occasionally more; most parts aromatic. Leaves always in opposite pairs, hairless, shiny mid-green above paler below, about 2.5-4cm long, usually widest at or below the middle; veins obscure. Flowers 2-3cm wide, smelling of sour milk (or sweet-smelling depending on one's interpretation). Fruit a berry, blue-black when ripe usually a little longer than wide; flesh green, many small seeds. Edible.

Flowering: June to August, September in the hills.

Habitat: Open rocky ground, with other shrubs in heathlands, near streams and in seasonally muddy ground, under pine and oak woods. Lowlands to mountains.

Distribution: Mainly western Mediterranean region, Portugal, North Africa.

Family: Eucalyptus family, Myrtaceae.

Notes: Because of the essential oil present in the leaves, Myrtle was known to the ancient Greeks and Romans. Country people in southern Spain use the leaves to alleviate colds and bronchitis and the dried berries for flavouring. There is a small-leaved form in the Alhambra gardens in Granada that is considered distinct.

AMMI MAJUS **False Bishop's Weed,** Ami vulgár.

Description: Tall slender annual to 1.50m. Superficially like Wild Carrot, but is hairless. Branches many, slender and spreading. Leaves blue-green, divided twice into relatively wider leaflets. Compare with A. *visnaga* (p.98) and *Daucus carota* (p.102), leaflets with serrate margins. Flowers many, tiny, chalk-white in small heads forming a large, flat and open flowerhead about 8-12cm diameter, each on long slender stalklets. At the main base is a collar of finely divided bracts. Seed heads in open slender rays.

Flowering: From about April to July.

Habitat: Common in dry fields, roadsides and other open places from the coast to about 700m.

Distribution: A Mediterranean species; Portugal.

Family: Carrot and Fennel family, Umbelliferae (Apiaceae).

Notes: A good butterfly plant and worthy of cultivation apart from being a host of blackfly.

AMMI VISNAGA, **Ammi,** Bisnaga.

Description: A stout yellowish-green annual about 1m tall. Compare with A.*majus* (p.97). Leaves pinnate in the lowest, but others cut into very fine pale- green fennel-like leaflets. Flowers very small white and grouped into a head which is conspicuously rounded on top (like a minature old-fashioned parachute). Bracts below flowerhead are very finely cut and hang down close to the stem. Seedheads become thickened and close up when ripe.

Flowering: Later than A.*majus*, about June to August.

Habitat: Throughout southern Spain, often covering a field in close stands, and is most conspicuous.

Distribution: Widely spread Mediterranean species; Portugal.

Family: Carrot and Fennel family, Umbelliferae (Apiaceae).

Notes: In cooler places it can become a troublesome weed covering wide areas. Is sometimes used by country people in Spain as a diuretic and to relieve asthma.

BUPLEURUM FRUTICOSUM, **Shrubby Thorow-wax,** Adelfilla.

Description: Shrub, 2m or more with erect pale branches. Leaves tough in texture, with a translucent margin, reaching the main veins. Flowers in open heads, rays up to 25; yellow.

Flowering: June to August.

Habitat: Rocks and dry rubbly places, usually limestone; low hills to mountains, commonly in open places.

Distribution: Southern Europe, North Africa.

Family: Carrot and Fennel family, Umbelliferae (Apiaceae).

Notes: The plant is conspicuous even when not in flower; it is commonly seen on the hills behind Estepona to Malaga. A very closely related species, B.*gibraltarium* (generally spelled in some books *gibraltaricum*) differs mainly in that the leaf-veining does not reach the margin and the pale marginal vein is absent. It is common in the hills and mountains to the east, but strangely does not occur on Gibraltar, where the other species is common.

BUPLEURUM LANCIFOLIUM, **Hare's-ear, Thorow-wax,**
Perfoliata.

Description: Annual, soft and hairless, small, usually less
than 50cm high, pale green, branched. Leaves, only the basal
rather narrow and tapered, the upper surround the stem
(perfoliate). Flowers in heads (umbels) of 3-5 surrounded by
yellow bracts which fade dull yellow. Fruits, small oblong covered
with little tubercules, remain on the plant, darkening with
maturity.

Flowering: April to June, but dead plants remaining intact
until late July.

Habitat: Mainly grassy fields and cultivated land with loose
tilled soil; easily overlooked.

Distribution: Southern Europe, North Africa; occasionally
cultivated.

Family: Carrot and Fennel family, Umbelliferae (Apiaceae).

Notes: Heads dry well and are attractive in small floral arrangements.
A diverse genus, there are other small annual species, but also some
low-growing perennials with tough grass-like leaves; common in
limestone.

CONIUM MACULATUM, **Hemlock,** Ceguta (or Ciguta).

Description: Soft annual or biennial, tall erect to about 2m; main stem hollow, smooth and hairless with a "bloom" and purplish-red markings; many branches above. Leaves green and shiny, large but cut into segments about 4 times (4 pinnate), ultimate margins saw-toothed. Flowers very small in stalked heads; about 7-12 or more of these comprising a large head. Fruit dry, oval in outline, about 1cm long, but nearly flat with narrow wavy ridges.

Flowering: May to July.

Habitat: Mainly damp places, stream and river sides, damp ditches on road edges; also on banks in soft soil but then usually above 300m.

Distribution: Nearly all of Europe, North Africa.

Family: Carrot and Fennel family, Umbelliferae (Apiaceae).

Notes: The strong mouse smell of the plant helps in identification. All parts of this plant are extremely poisonous, seeds especially so. Well known as the poison that killed Socrates, who recorded the progress of this nerve poison as his limbs became devoid of feeling. Today, the main deaths are from cattle eating the plant growing amongst pastures; apparently it loses the poison when dry so that hay should be safe.

DAUCUS CAROTA, **Wild Carrot,** Acenoria, Zanahoria silvestre.

Description: Erect annual or biennial with several distinct forms (sub-species); height from a few centimetres to over a metre. Most parts covered with short stiff hairs; stalks thin, one to three. Leaves divided into finely-cut narrow leaflets; flowers white, tiny and grouped into a flattish head (umbel) about 10-20 or even up to 35cm wide, with a collar of finely-cut lacy bracts beneath the umbel. Distinctive is a blackish-purple and rather fleshy flower (or flowers) in the centre of a head. This may be missing in some sub-species. Fruits are small, dryish and prickly, less than half a centimetre long. When fruits are mature the head closes up.

Flowering: From about April to early summer.

Habitat: Common on roadsides, fields and rough ground in open places.

Distribution: Throughout southern Spain.   Throughout Europe.

Family: Carrot and Fennel family, Umbelliferae (Apiaceae).

Notes: An attractive form (ssp. *hispanicus*) has very large heads which do not close up in fruit. A coastal plant. Flowers of Wild Carrot have a dusty scent which attracts butterflies. Plants were used for medicine by the ancient Europeans.

ERYNGIUM DILATATUM, Eryngo azul

Description: Perennial herb not more than 40cm high, spiny, texture tough. Leaves lobed, a few basal on stems deeply divided with fairly soft spines. Flowers on erect stems, very small, crowded into heads, each head surrounded by 5-10 narrow and spiny bracts.

Flowering: June to September.

Habitat: Dry heathlands, fields and amongst *Cistus* bushes and other shrubs in rocky ground; frequent; lowlands to mid hills.

Distribution: Spain, Portugal, North Africa.

Family: Carrot and Fennel family, Umbelliferae (Apiaceae).

Notes: There are several similar species in our area not easy to distinguish. E.*tricuspidatum* of similar habitat and as common, is a slender perennial with very thin segments around the head; basal leaves are wide and unlobed. They are closely related to the robust Sea Holly, E.*maritimum,* of coastal sands throughout much of Europe.

***FERULA COMMUNIS*, Giant Fennel,** Cañaferla.

Description: Very tall erect perennial, about 3-4m with one thick, round stem. Leaves huge, basal, dark green and cut into fine, fennel-like segments which are strongly scented when dry. Flowers yellow, very small but in large compound heads at the ends of branchlets; flowers scented. Seeds (mericarps) elliptic but flat, each just over a centimetre long.

Flowering: Late March to June.

Habitat: Hills and mountains in southern Spain, mainly limestone but at sea-level near Sanlúcar (Cádiz); also in meadows which are damp in winter amongst mountains behind the Costa del Sol and near Jerez.

Distribution: Southern Spain and Mediterranean Europe, Portugal.

Family: Carrot and Fennel family, Umbelliferae (Apiaceae).

Notes: Takes 3 to 4 years to flower and is then conspicuous. Easily seen from the verandah of the Reina Victoria hotel at Ronda on the cliff edge over the valley. The dried pith of the stem was used in the past for torches and parts of the plant produce a medicinal gum. Some of the *Ferula* species are used in modern heart medicine. Another, F.*tingitana*, grows on Gibraltar's rock slopes. It has similar flowers but more coarsely cut shiny leaves.

THAPSIA GARGANICA, **Giant Thapsia,** Tapsia, Asa dulce.

Description: Perennial over 2m high with tough basal fibres; stem erect, solid, round and smooth. Leaves, basal about 40 x 20cm, 2-3 pinnate, pale to mid-green, whitish beneath. Flowerheads hairless without bracts at the bases. Fruit in stalked heads, each about 2.5cm long with wide papery wings.

Flowering: March to July, August in the mountains.

Habitat: Most commonly in limestone areas, rocks and crevices and rough slopes; low hills to mountains.

Distribution: Southern Mediterranean region, Portugal.

Family: Carrot and Fennel family, Umbelliferae (Apiaceae).

Notes: There are two other species of *Thapsia* in southern Spain and one, T. *maxima* is about the same height, but has coarser leaves divided only once (pinnate). See also Ferula (p.104). Giant Thapsia, though it contains an irritant resin, has been used as a purgative from remote times and is described in Dioscorides' Materia Medica. The famous North African drug Silphium, of the ancients, was probably related to *Thapsia* or *Ferula tingitana,* but became extinct about 7th Century, A.D.

ARBUTUS UNEDO, **Strawberry Tree,** Madroño.

Description: Evergreen, woody shrub or tree, up to 9m; bark light red, rough. Leaves alternate, tough and shiny, margins slightly toothed. Flowers small, in clusters, cream petals, fused together and nipped in at the apex. Fruits, edible, nobbly and soft, nearly 3cm across, ripening scarlet. They take about a year to ripen so that flowers and fruits are on the tree at the same time.

Flowering: October to December, occasionally to January.

Habitat: In rocky ground, light woods associated with corkwoods (*Quercus suber*) in the west and further east with Encina or Holm Oak (Q. *ilex*). Also in open rocky hills, in sandstone in the west, less commonly perhaps, in limestone; all through southern Spain.

Distribution: Southern Spain; a Mediterranean species, Portugal, Northwest Ireland.

Family: Heather and Rhododendron family, Ericaceae.

Notes: There is only one species in Spain and it was much cut in the past for its wood which was used mainly for making charcoal. Leaves were used medicinally and are the food of the caterpillar of the large and rather rare Two-tailed Pasha butterfly.

CALLUNA VULGARIS, **Ling, Heather,** Brecina.

Description: A perennial spreading bush, very small to over a metre; flowering when only a few centimetres high if in leached or poor soil. Leaves very small; flowers small in spikes at the end of twigs, the colour varying from very pale to a deep pink.

Flowering: Varies from late July to December, occasionally into January. The remains (the calyx) of old flowers are on plants for most of the year, resembling flowers.

Habitat: Typically in sandstone and neutral soils, corkwoods and in open places on hillsides and stony ground, low altitudes to at least 700m.

Distribution: Widely spread throughout Europe, Portugal and in non-limestone areas of North Africa.

Family: . Heather and Rhododendron family, Ericaceae.

Notes: It is also a heather, but differs from the *Erica* species mainly; the leaves are much smaller, short and in opposite overlapping pairs (*Ericas* are in threes or more arising from one place on the stem). Also petals are small and hidden in the sepals which are pink and remain after the petals have fallen. This is the heath that forms the grouse moors of Scotland.

ERICA ARBOREA, **Tree Heather,** Brezo blanco.

Description: Large woody shrub to about 3m high (in our area) flowering from about 1.50m. Leaves in whorls of 3, occasionally 4, about 3-5mm long, linear with inrolled margins almost meeting. Flowers on upper twiglets, densely floriferous; corolla about 4mm long; anthers not protruding, basal appendages present (see E.*umbellata* p.112), finely hairy, style dark, longer than corolla.

Flowering: February to June, July in mountains.

Habitat: In deciduous oak, cork and pine woods, often by streams or in open places with other shrubs and amongst mossy rocks in hill forest; lowlands to mountains at least 650m., preferring non-limestone.

Distribution: Widely spread in Mediterranean areas, Portugal, and North Africa, reaching as far as Abyssinia.

Family: Heather and Rhododendron family, Ericaceae.

Notes: Distinguished by its height and pure white flowers with dark style. It is the same species as the Tree Heath of the Azores which grows to about 7m and has a substantial trunk.

ERICA AUSTRALIS, Southern Heather, Brezo colorada, Perrita.

Description: Slender shrub with erect branches to 2m. Leaves in whorls, each of four, 3-6mm long with margins rolled under. Flowers in lax clusters with comparatively long bells, about 6-9mm; style protruding but usually not the stamens; anthers with toothed appendages, (see E.*umbellata* p.112).

Flowering: December to April - June in the mountains.

Habitat: Calcifuge; frequently forming thickets in scrubland or on open neutral soils, rocky hillsides and in open cork and pine woods; lowlands to over 1,000m in the mountains in non-limestone pockets, i.e. Sierras de Ronda.

Distribution: Spain, southern Portugal, North Africa.

Family: Heather and Rhododendron family, Ericaceae.

Notes: A fairly easy species to distinguish from the other heathers in our area and one of the most attractive with a long flowering period.

ERICA CILIARIS, **Dorset Heath,** Agaña, Carroncha.

Description: Small spreading shrublet with weak branches and usually less than 1m in height. Leaves glandular on the margins. Flowers comparatively large for heathers (1cm long) in erect terminal racemes; stamens have no flap-like appendages (see E. *umbellata* p.112) and are shorter than the lip of the flower.

Flowering: About late July to October or November.

Habitat: Damp open places; in light corkwoods, streamsides in acid soils; lowlands to hills in the southwest, less commonly in the east of our area.

Distribution: Western Europe, North Africa, in acid soils.

Family: Heather and Rhododendron family, Ericaceae.

Notes: Distinguished from other heathers here by the large flowers, few to a head. There are four other species in southern Spain that tolerate damp habitats. The spring flowering, tall white-flowered E.*arborea* with a dark stigma protruding and E.*lusitanica* with a pink stigma with appendages on the stamens (use lens) often grow near streams. (See E. *umbellata* p.112).

***ERICA SCOPARIA*, Green Heather,** Brezo de escobas.

Description: Tall erect shrub to about 1-2m high. Leaves in whorls of 3-4; margins inrolled nearly meeting underneath. Flowers pale green or partly to wholly dull pink, corolla short and wide not more than 3mm long; stamens, terracotta colour, just reaching the edge of corolla-lobes; anthers without basal appendages (see E. *umbellata* p.112).

Flowering: March to June.

Habitat: Abundant in open dry scrubland, heaths and often mixed with other species of *Erica* and *Calluna* on hillsides and in corkwoods; mainly lowlands but to at least 650m in mountains; calcifuge.

Distribution: Southwest Europe, North Africa; in southern Spain most frequent in the southwest, but widely distributed.

Family: Heather and Rhododendron family, Ericaceae.

Notes: It is not always easy to see when the plants are in bloom even though the anthers are conspicuous. When ripe, the pollen is blown out by wind shaking the bush and a cloud of greeny-cream pollen erupts over it and is visible before being blown away.

ERICA UMBELLATA, **Cluster Heather,** Brezo.

Description: Small woody shrub to about 80cm high but often flowering when about 15cm. Leaves linear, less than 3mm long in whorls of three, margins inrolled. Flowers terminal or twigs in loose bunches, each flower about 5cm long with erect lobes, narrowed where the dark stamens protrude. Anthers without appendages; flowers vary from pale to dark pink.

Flowering: February to July.

Habitat: In open corkwoods, heaths and leached acid or neutral soil amongst bare rocks; calcifuge.

Distribution: Southwest Spain, southern Portugal, North Africa.

Family: Heather and Rhododendron family, Ericaceae.

Notes: Nearly all our heathers are lime haters (calcifuge) but may be found in pockets surrounded by limestone. For instance, below the limestone massif of Grazalema a lot of heathers occur for several hectares. Here are corkwoods and *Cistus ladanifer,* both of which indicate the absence of lime. Of the seven species of heather in our area, four have little earlike appendages on the anthers which help in identification.

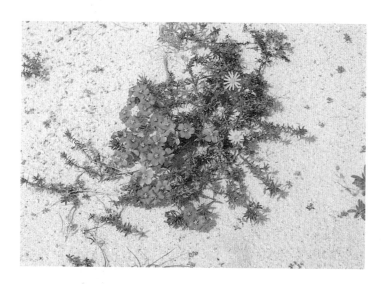

ANAGALLIS MONELLI, **Large Pimpernel,** Murajes de lino.

Description: Low growing perennial or biennial herb with stems about 30cm high; much branched. Leaves variable but mostly linear. Flowers large, to 3cm across with the centre either rose-red or light purple, occasionally white or almost all blue, stalks thin; flowers opening in the sun.

Flowering: January to October, but mainly between February and July.

Habitat: In sand and other light soils, open places and shrubby ground, edges of country roadsides; coastal to hills.

Distribution: Spain, Portugal, Mediterranean islands (Sardinia and Sicily).

Family: Primula family, Primulaceae.

Notes: The common small red Pimpernel of Europe is frequently blue-flowered here and looks like a minature of the above. The yellow daisy in the plate is *Senecio gallicus,* common on coastal sands.

***OLEA EUROPAEA* var. *SYLVESTRIS,* Wild Olive,** Acebuche.

Description: Tree, 10-15m high if left to grow, but mainly seen as a shrub or small tree, or sometimes densely branched with hard interleaving twigs resembling spines. Bark whitish at first ageing to dark grey and fissured; wood dense and extremely hard. Leaves dark green above, paler and felty beneath; between 2-8cm long. Flowers cream, fading darker, scented. Fruit a drupe (like a plum), pale green ripening blackish-purple, small in the wild form, usually less than 2cm long.

Flowering: Mainly May and June; good flowering occuring about every 5-6 years, but otherwise every two years.

Habitat: Abundant in all types of soil, rocky places, woods etc; lowlands to mid mountains.

Distribution: Mediterranean area, Portugal, North Africa.

Family: Jasmine and Ash family, Oleaceae.

Notes: The cultivar (var. *europaea*) produces much larger, round to oblong fruits and the plant is distinguished by its leaves which are silver in comparison; the trunk often shows the graft wound. Fruits need to be treated first in brine before eating unless they are to be crushed for oil. A very important tree to man and has been in use for thousands of years. Trees are very long-lived, some reputed to be at least 1,000 years old.

CENTAURIUM ERYTHRAEA, ssp. GRANDIFLORUM, **Common Centuary,** Hiel de tierra, Cintoria.

Description: Small erect biennial herb commonly 20-30cm tall, with one to several flowering stems. Leaves shiny, hairless with 3-7 distinct veins; the basal leaves in a loose rosette, those on the stem in opposite pairs. Flowers about 2cm across with blunt petals; in flattish heads.

Flowering: April to July, sometimes until autumn.

Habitat: Common in open places, often sandy soil, light woodlands, grassy roadsides, lowlands and hills.

Distribution: All of Europe with several species in southern Spain.

Family: Gentian family, Gentianaceae.

Notes: A variable plant divided into three sub-species common in our area; ssp. *majus* has brilliant magenta-pink flowers of the same size in large heads and flowers from about May. The other, ssp. *erythraea* is pale pink or sometimes white with smaller flowers and pointed petals. There are other species in this area and a common one is the smaller C. *maritimum* with a few pale yellow flowers.

NERIUM OLEANDER, **Oleander,** Adelfa.

Description: Woody bushes, usually 1-4m tall; most parts very poisonous. Leaves tough, hairless, mid to dark green above, and paler below; shape narrow and about 20-23cm long. Flowers about 4cm wide, almond scented especially at night. Pods long, dark brown splitting open, seeds with soft hairs.

Flowering: May to October.

Habitat: In our area confined to riversides and streams in open places and also in the shade of tall deciduous trees (Alders etc.) in woods of the lowlands.

Distribution: Mediterranean region, Portugal; commonly cultivated.

Family: Oleander family, Apocynaceae.

Notes: The scent at night attracts moths to nectar in the narrow tubes of the flowers. This is reached by the moth's long proboscis and ensures cross fertilisation. There is also another species cultivated in southern Spain which is native to India. Although extremely poisonous, Oleander has been used in medicines for many centuries.

VINCA DIFFORMIS, **Periwinkle,** Alcandórea.

Description: Low herb almost hairless, rooting at intervals where it produces erect but weak flowering stems sometimes very long. Leaves about 3.5-7cm long, in opposite pairs, hairless. Flowers solitary in a leaf axil with a tapering tube and the flat flower-part 3-4.5cm across, the lobes obliquely angled; commonly bright blue, but in our area often washed-out blue, or pure white.

Flowering: December to May or longer.

Habitat: Uncultivated land, under bushes, by streams in woods or in crevices in limestone hills, very common.

Distribution: Southwest Europe, sometimes naturalised elsewhere.

Family: Oleander family, Apocynaceae.

Notes: Some species are used medicinally, though possibly poisonous, and cattle avoid eating them. Two other species occur here, the darker blue V.*major* and V.*minor*, but not so commonly in our area.

PUTORIA CALABRICA, Hedionda

Description: Mat-forming perennial. Leaves small, usually about 2cm long, foul-smelling, leathery, hairy or not, in opposite pairs, stipulate. Flowers seldom more than 2cm long, pink with a tube and 4 lobes with stamens projecting; many together.

Flowering: July to September or October.

Habitat: Dry banks, rocky ground, roadsides, commonly in limestone areas from coast to mountains, excluding southwest lowlands.

Distribution: Most of Mediterranean Europe, common in southern Spain.

Family: Madder and Bedstraw family, Rubiaceae.

Notes: Most conspicuous in flower hanging over steep banks in mats looking so lovely, but the smell is terrible. The botanical name is very apt as it comes from *putor*, Latin for a foul smell.

CONVOLVULUS ALTHAEOIDES, **Mallow-leaved Bindweed,** Campanilla de Canarias.

Description: Perennial herb with short or long twining stems, 50-100cm, sometimes flat and bushy. Leaves stalked, dull and hairy with rather frilly margins and variable in shape, lowest usually unlobed, deeply heart-shaped at the base, upper variously lobed. Flowers pale to bright pink, about 5cm wide.

Flowering: April to June and July in the hills.

Habitat: Open places, dry and stony ground, rock faces, most types of soils.

Distribution: Widespread in the Mediterranean area, Portugal; abundant in southern Spain, coastal to mountains.

Family: Bindweed family, Convolvulaceae.

Notes: There is a sub-species, *tenuissima* which is an eastern Mediterranean form; slender with deeply lobed leaves, approaching some of our plants. It is especially common in Greece and Turkey, but not known in our area.

ANCHUSA AZUREA, **Blue Alkanet,** Lengua de buey, Lenguaza.

Description: A perennial herb with open flowering branches; most parts rough with hispid hairs which may have enlarged bases. Leaves dull, rather dark green rough with white hairs; basal largest. Flowers bright blue each about 1.5 to 2.5cm across, many out at one time.

Flowering: March to May.

Habitat: Open fields, roadside banks, especially but not always in limestone areas. Common from lowlands to the higher hills.

Distribution: Widely spread in Europe; North Africa.

Family: Forget-me-not family, Boraginaceae.

Notes: Plants sometimes behave as annuals or more commonly as biennials, particularly in non-limestone soils. There are references in old books as a medicinal plant which may have been confused with the better known Borage (*Borago officinalis*), an annual also with bright blue flowers and roughly hairy leaves and stem. It has been used in country medicine and in salads for centuries. Flowers of *Anchusa* species are not scented but the leaves are when dried.

BORAGO OFFICINALIS, **Borage,** Borraja común.

Description: Annual to about 70cm, branched with hollow stems; all parts except petals covered with short, sharp and pale hairs. Leaves with puckered surface (bullate), variable in size; basal sometimes to 25cm long and stalked; stem leaves stalkless. Flowers on short bent stalks, almost scentless, gentian-blue.

Flowering: February to May.

Habitat: Country roadsides, seasonally damp fields in sandy or rubbly soil; often cultivated; lowlands mainly.

Distribution: Southern Europe, but a garden escape and naturalised in other European countries.

Family: Forget-me-not family, Boraginaceae.

Notes: A good honey flower; despite the unpleasant hairs leaves are used in cooking and flowers used fresh are attractive in green salads tasting of cucumber. Borage has also been used as a heart tonic and is in very old herb books (called Bugloss by Dioscorides).

CERINTHE MAJOR, **Honeywort,** Ceriflor.

Description: Soft annual herb, stems about 20-50cm high, hairless, leaves pale green, blunt at the apex. Flowers about 1.5-3cm long, tubular, usually dark purplish-red but sometimes dark cream with a red ring near the base.

Flowering: February to April or early May.

Habitat: Fields and meadows, grassy road verges, waste places; coastal to hills.

Distribution: Mediterranean area, Portugal.

Family: Forget-me-not family, Boraginaceae.

Notes: An unusual-looking flower easily recognised. The English name is because of the honey scent of the nectar in the tube, which makes it a good bee plant. Some *Cerinthe* with cream or yellow flowers may be a sub-species (recently re-established as a species, C.*gymnandra*).

***ECHIUM ALBICANS*, White-leaved Bugloss,** Viborera.

Description: Erect greyish perennial to about 80cm high; one to several main stems. Leaves basal, in a rosette, stem leaves narrower with rather soft silvery-white hairs. Flowers to about 2.5cm long, pink to blue-pink; calyx with long narrow and hairy segments; some stamens longer than the corolla.

Flowering: April or May to July.

Habitat: A lime-loving plant growing amongst rocks in hill-sides and in roadside rubble in open places; commonly above 650m to about 1,800m.

Distribution: Endemic in limestone areas to the high hills and mountains of southern Spain.

Family: Forget-me-not family, Boraginaceae.

Notes: Flowers attract mountain butterflies. This species could be confused with another, slightly taller (to 100cm) and much branched biennial (E.*asperrimum*) which has harsh hairs and paler flowers. It has a wider range in Spain and occurs also in France and Italy, as well as in North Africa.

ECHIUM BOISSIERI, Candle Bugloss.

Description: Tall erect biennial with one long and narrow flowering stem, about 2m high in the second year. Leaves blue-green, dull and hispid with pale hairs, forming a basal rosette during the first year and the tall flowering spike the second year, with smaller narrow leaves amongst the flowers on the lower part. Flowers many, small, about 1.5cm long, pale pink widening at the apex, with staminal filaments of uneven lengths, longer than the flower.

Flowering: May and June.

Habitat: Open ground on dry banks in rubbly soil on roadsides mainly acid or neutral, occasionally in limestone places (Ronda etc.).

Distribution: Southern Spain, Portugal, North Africa.

Family: Forget-me-not family, Boraginaceae.

Notes: The plant dies after flowering, but the dead spike remains erect for some months. A few plants grow on the steep limestone cliffs on the east side of Gibraltar.

ECHIUM PLANTAGINEUM, **Purple Bugloss,** Viborera.

Description: Biennial (occasionally annual), less than 1m tall, erect and branched, nearly all parts hairy. Basal leaves to about 15 x 5cm; stem leaves smaller and narrow, slightly heart-shaped at base with prominent veins and appressed hairs. Flowers mainly on branched stemlets; calyx to 1cm; flowers about 3cm long, hairy only on the veins and margins; two stamens slightly exserted from lip of corolla.

Flowering: March to June.

Habitat: From lowlands to hills, very common in sand and open fields; often forming masses in grassy fields, roadsides, etc. Throughout our area.

Distribution: Widespread in warmer countries of Europe; North Africa; naturalised in others.

Family: Forget-me-not family, Boraginaceae.

Notes: Called E. *lycopsis* in some books. Difficult to distinguish from some of the other blue-flowered species. The common Viper's Bugloss (E.*vulgare*) has several stamens extended beyond the corolla which is hairy on the outside.

***LITHODORA FRUTICOSA*, Limestone Gromwell,** Asperones.

Description: Spreading to almost erect woody herb growing to about 60cm; branches and twigs bristly (setose), whitish when young. Leaves narrow, rough with appressed hairs with thickened bases; margins rolled under. Flowers with pinkish tube especially when young; hairless except on the outside of the corolla lobes.

Flowering: March to August.

Habitat: Dry and stony ground, edges of roadsides, usually limestone areas.

Distribution: Spain, France, North Africa. In southern Spain, rare in the southwest but common elsewhere from lowlands to hills.

Family: Forget-me-not family, Boraginaceae.

Notes: Previously called *Lithospermum fruticosum.* It is replaced in the southwest by L.*diffusa* with gentian-blue flowers. Hairs are somewhat softer and the corolla is hairy on the outside; the tube is not pink and the plant hates limestone. It grows amongst heathers and in light corkwoods.

OMPHALODES COMMUTATA, **Navel-wort,** Carmelita.

Description: Annual, slender, erect. Leaves stalkless except for some basal; about 3.5cm long. Flowers each about 8mm wide. Nutlets hairless, each surrounded by a narrow entire wing.

Flowering: April to June.

Habitat: Commonly amongst limestone, in crevices or in grassy ground below cliffs, dry places; many growing together; mountains.

Distribution: Southern Spain, North Africa; usually above 400m.

Family: Forget-me-not family, Boraginaceae.

Notes: Previously called O. *brassicifolia.* There is a similar species with which it may be confused, also an annual, O. *linifolia.* Leaves are narrow, flowers may have a slightly blue tinge, nutlets are hairy and the wing has a scalloped (crenate) margin. It is more common in the lowlands and hills.

***VITEX AGNUS-CASTUS*, Chaste Tree,** Gatillo casto, Agnocasto.

Description: A rather open shrub or small tree about 3-4m high; twigs felted, whitish. Leaves aromatic, cut to base into long sharp-pointed lobes, white felted underneath. Flowers many, small, from pale to mid-lilac (deep lilac in the southwest).

Flowering: July to early October.

Habitat: Lowlands, by rivers and streamsides, damp open places often together with Oleander (p.116)

Distribution: Mediterranean Europe, Portugal. Often cultivated.

Family: Verbena and Lantana family, Verbenaceae.

Notes: A plant of ancient usage producing over the centuries, a yellow dye, medicine for heart and stomach, twigs for weaving and fruits for seasoning (locally called Monks' Pepper-tree). The name is from *castus* Latin for purity and *agnus* a lamb, suggesting innocence.

AJUGA CHAMAEPITYS, **Ground Pine,** Pinillo oloroso.

Description: Small spreading and much branched herb, usually an annual and about 10-30cm high. Leaves hairless to densely covered with fine pale hairs; very narrow and divided into 3 long, linear segments - not always apparent; margins entire (un-notched). Flowers about 1.5cm long, two-lipped but upper is so short that it may appear to be absent; lower lip lobed, yellow with fine purplish marks near the throat; stamens protruding, filaments hairy.

Flowering: April to June.

Habitat: Dry stony ground, sloping fields and arid areas.

Distribution: Widespread in Europe, especially in Mediterranean countries; North Africa. In our area mainly in hills and mountains.

Family: Mint family, Labiatae (Lamiaceae).

Notes: Quite unlike other little plants; the pale leaves have a strong pine-like smell, and it has been used medicinally for centuries and appears in the Materia Medica of Dioscorides published in the 2nd century AD.

CALAMINTHA SYLVATICA, **Wood Calamint,** Calamenta, (Southern Andalucia: Hierba pastora).

Description: Aromatic, slender perennial, short-lived, becoming woody and spreading but if amongst other growth may be up to 50-60cm high; all parts hairy except for flowers. Leaves with shallowly scalloped (crenate) margins. Flowers in loose whorls 9-10 together, each stalk shorter than the calyx; flowers pale pink to lilac-pink with darker markings on lower lip. Calyx with 2 elongated teeth.

Flowering: October to February.

Habitat: In rough dry or seasonally damp places, edges of light woods in sandy ground, very common.

Distribution: Western and southern Europe, North Africa.

Family: Mint family, Labiatae (Lamiaceae).

Notes: Another species, C. *nepeta,* is very similar but has up to 20 flowers in each whorl, each flower stalk as long as the calyx, the 2 calyx teeth only slightly elongated. Little separates the two species and they appear to hybridise as well, showing features of both. A tisane is made for stomach complaints and it was wound around the neck to combat a cold (there seems sense in this, as one would inhale the soothing balm from this strongly aromatic herb).

LAVANDULA DENTATA, **Toothed Lavender,** Alhucema rizada.

Description: Small grey-green perennial shrub about 1m wide and high, densely leafy. All parts pleasantly aromatic and covered with greyish pubescence of minute matted hairs. Leaves stalkless, to 5cm long but less than 1cm wide, deeply cut into close and evenly rounded lobes. Flowers tiny, pale lilac, are in a flowerhead about 4-5cm long which is widest at the base with a topknot of pinkish-lilac, bracts 1.5-2cm long.

Flowering: February to June, or July in the hills.

Habitat: Mainly amongst limestone rocks, occasionally in dry neutral soils, but locally common and absent from wide areas.

Distribution: Italy, Spain, cultivated in Portugal and other Mediterranean countries. Common on the rock of Gibraltar, and very common in gardens.

Family: Mint family, Labiatae (Lamiaceae).

Notes: This species does not seem to be used in perfumery nor for medicine, but its flowers are rich in nectar which is collected by bees and made into excellent honey. In southern Spain there is an attractive grey-leaved form in cultivation.

LAVANDULA MULTIFIDA, **Cut-leaved Lavender,** Alhucemilla.

Description: Greyish small straggly shrub or perennial herb with an unpleasant tar-like smell in all parts; hairy. Usually less than 50cm tall, but in good soil can have stems to a metre long. Leaves pale grey to grey-green, up to 5 x 5cm but divided finely into leaflets, which are toothed. Stems pale green with spreading hairs. Flowers in thin heads, and without the coloured topknot of other species, are on very long bare stalks and sometimes there are 3 heads; individual flowers are comparatively large, about 1.5cm long.

Flowering: Most of the year.

Habitat: Mainly amongst limestone and arid soil.

Distribution: Spain, Italy, Portugal, North Africa. A common species in southern Spain apart from the extreme southwest; frequent on Gibraltar.

Family: Mint family, Labiatae (Lamiaceae).

Notes: Its very strong unpleasant smell contradicts the idea of a Lavender plant, so seems to be the black sheep of this genus and not even used medicinally. Even its shape is unattractive as branches tend to spread untidily except in coastal sands where it is more compact.

LAVANDULA STOECHAS, **French Lavendar,** Cantueso, Azaya.

Description: Small woody perennial shrublet of several distinct forms and from a few cm high to 60cm, usually depending on the soil; all parts pleasantly aromatic. Leaves pale to mid green, softly hairy, pointed and with entire margins. Flowers in elongated heads about 3-4 x 1.75cm, oval to oblong and often slightly wider at the base; topped by purple to lilac or pink bracts varying in shape and length from about 1cm to 2.5cm long with wavy margins in the well-defined sub-species. Flowers are tiny and usually purple.

Flowering: Nearly all the year.

Habitat: Very common in sandy and acid soils; also in limestone areas, in light woods or open places amongst larger shrubs.

Distribution: Mediterranean Europe, Portugal.

Family: Mint family, Labiatae (Lamiaceae).

Notes: During the intense heat of summer the pleasant aroma gets an overlying goaty smell. It is a very old medicinal herb and its essential oil was used here especially as an antiseptic for washing wounds. The most distinct sub-species of L.*stoechas* is *sampaiana* endemic to Spain. The bare stalks of the flowerheads are very long and the bracts of the topknot are at least 3cm long with wavy margins, but there are many intermediates, difficult to separate.

133

MENTHA PULEGIUM, **Pennyroyal,** Poleo.

Description: Aromatic perennial herb; young plants flat and creeping, hairless but when mature have erect stems and are hairy, to about 40cm. Leaves variable 3-4cm long; when young shiny and hairless but when flowering leaves are covered with short pale hairs and leaf margins curl upwards; very strong-smelling. Flowers vary from pale lilac to white.

Flowering: June to September.

Habitat: Grassy fields, open places in seasonally damp ground and on streamside banks in light woods. Abundant, lowlands to hills.

Distribution: Most of Europe, North Africa.

Family: Mint family, Labiatae (Lamiaceae).

Notes: There are three other native species in our area but only the wild form of Applemint (M.*suaveolens*) is common; there are hybrids and other species in cultivation and all possess essential oil in their leaves. Pennyroyal is used in Spain mainly in a tisane to induce sleep and a flowering twig placed behind each ear is most effective in keeping off biting insects.

PHLOMIS LYCHNITIS, **Yellow Phlomis,** Candilera, Torcida de candil.

Description: Woody herb growing to about half a metre. Leaves soft, grey and almost white on the underside with felted hairs. Erect flowering stems; flowers rich yellow.

Flowering: Spring and early summer, to July in high mountains.

Habitat: In dry and rocky limestone hills and mountains from about 500m., from near Gaucin eastwards and abundant in the Ronda hills; occasionally in lowlands amongst limestone outcrops.

Distribution: Portugal, Spain, occasional in France.

Family: Mint family, Labiatae (Lamiaceae).

Notes: A beautiful plant showing very little variation, and flowering all at the same time within an area, covering hillsides. In the past, leaves were dried and twisted and used as wicks for candles and lamps. The yellow-flowered *Phlomis fruticosa* which is commonly cultivated in European gardens, is a widely spread Mediterranean native, but does not occur naturally in Spain. It tends to hybridize with P.*purpurea* (p.136) if grown together.

***PHLOMIS PURPUREA*, Jerusalem Sage,** Matagallo.

Description: A very common woody herb to sub-shrub up to 1.50m occasionally 2m. Leaves greyish-green, felted on the underside. Flowers on erect leafy stems, soft pink. All parts with a slight aromatic smell.

Flowering: From late February to June, or July in high altitudes.

Habitat: On almost any soil, from sandy coasts up to about 1,000m in open places, often forming large stands, especially amongst Gorse, Genistas and Lentisc. In poor soil it flowers when small.

Distribution: Portugal, Spain; throughout southern Spain.

Family: Mint family, Labiatae (Lamiaceae).

Notes: Sometimes used by foreigners for culinary Sage, but is a poor substitute. Previously used in Spain as a diuretic medicine. The new stems are covered with loose white felty fluff, which is eagerly sought by the entertaining little Carder Bees. They remove large mouthfuls for nests for their eggs, adding pollen and nectar for food after hatching.

PRASIUM MAJUS

Description: Small twiggy shrub about a metre high. Leaves shiny, dark green, commonly about 3-4cm long with crenate margins and heart-shaped at the bases. Flowers white, about 2cm long and 2-lipped, the lower lobed, the middle one largest; purple marks on the upper part. Nutlets almost fleshy, black.

Flowering: February to June.

Habitat: Dry ground, bushy places, clefts in rocks especially in limestone; never far from the sea.

Distribution: Throughout the Mediterranean area (but not mainland France); Portugal. Throughout our area.

Family: Mint family, Labiatae (Lamiaceae).

Notes: Very common on the limestone cliffs of Gibraltar, but rather rare in nearby Spain (associated with the dwarf palm on cliffs above the sea near Algeciras and on marine limestone near Tarifa). A seemingly unsung little shrub which does not seem to be in cultivation nor have any common name, yet it is attractive with the dark green and shiny leaves contrasting with startlingly white flowers amongst them. Twigs tend to die (see plate) remaining on the plant, which is unsightly, but this does not occur so much in good soil.

***ROSMARINUS OFFICINALIS*, Rosemary,** Romero.

Description: Woody much branched shrub either small and spreading or erect and over 2m high; branches light brown. Leaves aromatic, 2-4cm long, very narrow with margins turned under; shiny and hairless above, pale beneath. Flowers 1-1.5cm long, calyx downy; colour usually pale lilac to lilac-blue with darker veins, rarely dark blue or pure white.

Flowering: September to May.

Habitat: Abundant in limestone especially on the mountains of our area; also in sand in the lowlands; less commonly in the southwest (Algeciras) area, but is on Gibraltar.

Distribution: Mediterranean region, Portugal.

Family: Mint family, Labiatae (Lamiaceae).

Notes: Abundant in cultivation, especially the very dark blue, which probably came from Corsica or the Balearics where it is common on the Formentor peninsula. A pure white form grows on the Sierra Blanca behind Marbella, and is tall and erect.

***SALVIA SCLAREA,* Clary,** Almaro, Amaro.

Description: Tall biennial or short-lived perennial; stem to 1m or more, erect; some parts sticky with glandular hairs; aromatic. Leaves large, often 30cm long including stalk, softly hairy and wrinkled; heart-shaped at base. Flowers very pale pink to lilac-pink, bracts longer than a single flower, thin and pinkish; calyx with long thin teeth; flowers 2-3cm long, upper lip long and curved.

Flowering: June to July.

Habitat: Dry, stony and rough uncultivated ground, often in limestone (Grazalema) from 100m to mountains.

Distribution: Southern Europe, North Africa.

Family: Mint family, Labiatae (Lamiaceae).

Notes: Often cultivated; in the past was used in country medicine. Another species, S. *argentea,* also in our area, is similar with erect heads and very large leaves but has pure white flowers in separate bunches on the stem; the bracts are smaller and green.

***STACHYS OCYMASTRUM*, Mediterranean Woundwort.**

Description: Small hairy annual from about 15 to 35 cm in height; leaves softly hairy with toothed margins; pale green. Flowers cream to pale yellow, crowded on erect square stems. Occasionally there is a small red spot at the base of a flower. The calyx has long teeth covered with fine hairs.

Flowering: Spring and summer; from early April to July.

Habitat: Open fields frequently in heavy soils but also in sand where other growth is sparse or short, on banks, roadsides, etc., in large patches.

Distribution: Common throughout Mediterranean countries, all through southern Spain. Often conspicuous because of its gregarious habit.

Family: Mint family, Labiatae (Lamiaceae).

Notes: Both leaves and flowers have a faint unpleasant smell but are beloved by bees. Many species of *Stachys* have been used to heal wounds (are scar-forming), hence the English name.

TEUCRIUM FRUTICANS, **Tree Germander,** Olivilla

Description: Woody shrub growing to about 2m but often much less; twigs white felted, 4 angled. Leaves very short-stalked in opposite pairs, oblong and blunt, slightly downy above (often lost on old leaves), white felted below. Flowers usually two out at a time on a twig end; flower with one 5-lobed lip up to 2.5cm long, remainder of corolla absent; colour variable from pure white (rare) through pale lilac, pinkish or pale blue-lilac, rarely dark blue.

Flowering: January to June.

Habitat: A very common plant of the woods, heaths, thickets (matorral); coastal to mountains. Soil not important.

Distribution: West Mediterranean countries, Portugal, North Africa. Common throughout southern Spain.

Family: Mint family, Labiatae (Lamiaceae).

Notes: Typical of this genus is the absence of petals other than the lip, but see *Ajuga* (p.129). The commonest colours of this species are very pale lilac and almost white (which is the common form on Gibraltar). Frequently cultivated in southern Spain, especially the deep saphire-blue flowered form which comes from North Africa. It was first found near Rabat on a limestone shelf by the famous British gardener, Captain Collingwood Ingram, about 60 years ago and brought into cultivation.

TEUCRIUM SCORODONIA ssp. BAETICUM, **Wood Sage,** Escorodonia.

Description: Herb with a creeping root stock; commonly 50-60cm high. Leaves and stems with short rather curly hairs, other parts with glandular hairs; leaves crenately lobed. Flowers with lobed lip (see *Teucrium fruticans* p.141), white or cream; corolla tube almost hidden in the calyx.

Flowering: April to August.

Habitat: Usually in semi-shade and amongst mossy rocks in light woods and hilly country; mainly in non-limestone.

Distribution: (for the sub-species) Spain, mainly southwest; North Africa.

Family: Mint family, Labiatae (Lamiaceae).

Notes: There are 3 sub-species occuring in Spain. T. *scorodonia* is a British native. It is used in country medicine as a tonic against colds.

***THYMUS CAPITATUS (THYMBRA CAPITATA)*, Andalusia Thyme,**
Tomillo común.

Description: A much branched woody herb about 30cm high
to a shrub of 1.50m; shape rounded. Leaves small, margins
inrolled, aromatic. Flowers pink, varying from pale to deeper
lilac-pink, covering the rounded tops with small flowers.

Flowering: From summer to August, occasionally September.

Habitat: Mainly on limestone (but not on Gibraltar), from
the lowlands to mountains, abundant, except in the southwest
where it occurs less commonly.

Distribution: Southern Spain, Mediterranean, Portugal.

Family: Mint family, Labiatae (Lamiaceae).

Notes: This Thyme is called *Coridothymus* in some books, and now is
put under *Thymbra* which differs by having 10-20 calyx veins (13 in
Thymus). A good butterfly plant. Dried leafy twigs are sold in markets in
southern Spain and are used in cooking and for tisanes. The plant
produces Thymol, an essential oil and used medically for centuries,
though seldom cultivated by the Spanish. More recently the chemical
compounds of some Thymes have been found to kill certain harmful
bacilli.

THYMUS GRANATENSIS, **Granada Thyme,** Tomillo.

Description: A spreading herb often almost flat, distinctive with its large, deep rose pink flowers and bracts, each about 1cm long. Leaves are flat (without rolled margins), hairless except at the base.

Flowering: From about April to July, or August at high altitudes.

Habitat: A limestone plant common on rocks and in roadside rubble, open places, from about Grazalema and the Ronda mountains eastwards.

Distribution: Endemic to southern Spain

Family: Mint family, Labiatae (Lamiaceae).

Notes: An attractive plant with its relatively large flowers. Spain is rich in different kinds of Thyme but most have smaller flowers or are white. They are common on limestone and there is one on Gibraltar, an attractive white flowered species (T.*willdenowii*) which does not occur in Spain.

MANDRAGORA AUTUMNALIS, **Mandrake**, Mandragora.

Description: Stemless perennial. Leaves unlobed, dark green, in a loose basal rosette 30cm or more long. Flowers many, one to each stalk from the centre of the plant; colour varies from blue-lilac to pinkish, pale to fairly dark. Berries fleshy, almost round, shiny and ripening yellow; all parts poisonous.

Flowering: October to about December; fruits ripening in the new year.

Habitat: Open places frequently in heavy clay; roadside rubble; near the coast and into the hills (Grazalema).

Distribution: Mediterranean region (excluding France), Portugal, in southern Spain absent in the east.

Family: Potato family, Solanaceae.

Notes: Dies back during summer, the large tuber remaining deep under the soil. A famous and evil plant believed in mediaeval times to have magic qualities and animism because the forked tuber had a human shape. When pulled up it screamed and killed the collector. As the tuber is a pain-killer, aphrodisiac and trustworthy poison for enemies, a method was devised to extract it safely. A starving dog was used to pull out the screaming tuber and thus died. The Mandrake was then safe to be handled.

***ANTIRRHINUM GRANITICUM** ssp. **BOISSIERI**,* **White Snapdragon.**

Description: A variable perennial herb covered with glandular hairs; usually bushy, erect and freely branched. Leaves with glandular hair; upper alternate. Flowers large, nearly 4cm long, usually white without a yellow boss, but sometimes this is present or the flower is pale pink.

Flowering: Spring to summer.

Habitat: Limestone in open places, mainly stony ground over 400m.

Distribution: Southern Spain, especially southeast; Portugal.

Family: Linaria family, Scrophulariaceae.

Notes: There are two sub-species of A. *graniticum*, the other, a calcifuge is not in our area. In the past, it was considered that there were two distinct species, the other being A. *hispanicum*, but there were too many intermediates to maintain them.

ANTIRRHINUM MAJUS ssp., **Snapdragon,** Boca de dragón.

Description: Perennial, usually small bushes with weak stems but some sub-species grow to 1.50m; hairless to glandular-hairy. Leaves alternate to opposite on upper stems, usually hairless. Flowers in erect heads in varying shades of pink with a yellow or occasionally white boss at the entrance to the throat.

Flowering: Early April to summer, later in mountains, continuing until early autumn.

Habitat: Varied but most commonly in rocky places, banks and in limestone crevices. One, ssp. *tortuosum*, grows in neutral or acid soil in the southwest.

Distribution: Mainly a Mediterranean species but has become naturalised in many countries from the cultivated plants. There are 3 sub-species in southern Spain, but ssp. *majus* is more common north of our area.

Family: Linaria family, Scrophulariaceae.

Notes: The sub-species may be distinguished: *majus*: leaves 4-9 times as long as wide, upper ones alternate. *tortuosum*: leaves at least 9 times as long as wide, upper ones often opposite, inflorescence hairless. *cirrhigerum*: (sandy soil, coastal) southwest Spain, Portugal.

CHAENORHINUM VILLOSUM, Cliffhanger.

Description: Sticky hairy perennial, low growing with spreading or ascending stems to about 30cm and as wide as 60cm or more; hanging branches even longer. Leaves hairy, small and more or less oval with entire margins; basal with short stems and opposite each other; upper often stalkless and alternate especially by the flowers. Flowers mainly white tinged with pale pink, or occasionally all pale pink; veins on upper lip conspicuously purple or dark pink.

Flowering: April to July.

Habitat: Essentially a cliff plant and mainly on limestone, on steep sides and on ledges where it can hang down. From sea-level to hills and mountains.

Distribution: Southern Spain, southern France, North Africa; on Gibraltar cliffs but rare in nearby southwest Spain where it occurs only on outcrops of limestone but is very common in the remainder of our area.

Family: Linaria family, Scrophulariaceae.

Notes: Grows in similar localities as Putoria (p.118) and is a conspicuous plant when in flower. It is still common on steep banks and cliffs on the winding hill roads behind the coast.

***DIGITALIS OBSCURA*, Spanish Foxglove,** Crujia.

Description: Perennial herb or small shrub; Leaves in basal rosettes, narrow and entire, or with large teeth on the margins (ssp. *laciniata*). Flowers about 2-3cm long have a projecting lip; the flower stems may be as tall as one metre.

Flowering: Spring to early summer.

Habitat: Rocky ground, hills and mountainsides; edges of forests and in shelter of trees. Limestone and serpentine.

Distribution: Southern Spain from about Sierra Bermeja (behind Estepona) and Grazalema eastwards. Throughout Spain; North Africa.

Family: Linaria family, Scrophulariaceae.

Notes: Many plants in this family are partial parasites, depending to some extent for nourishment obtained from the roots of nearby plants and so are difficult to cultivate. Most species of *Digitalis* are poisonous. The heart drug comes from the purple Foxglove (D. *purpurea* p.150), which is common in southern Spain.

DIGITALIS PURPUREA, **Foxglove,** Calzónes de Zorra, Dedalera.

Description: Usually perennial herb but sometimes dying after flowering. Leaves dull, medium to grey green, mostly basal but alternate on the erect flowering stem which grows to about 1m high. Flowers pink each about 4-5cm long, usually finely hairy on the outside.

Flowering: April to June.

Habitat: Light woods, amongst mossy rocks, in light shade or thickets, mainly above 250m altitude; dislikes limestone.

Distribution: Southwest and central Europe, northwest Africa. In southern Spain commonest in the southwest corkwoods.

Family: Linaria family, Scrophulariaceae.

Notes: Very poisonous but an important drug that has been used as a heart stimulant for centuries. Pollinated by bumblebees who pull the flower down with their weight. Their noise is amplified when inside. There are several rather similar sub-species. One has white flowers (ssp. *heywoodii*) and is found as far east as Jaen province.

LINARIA AMETHYSTEA, **Spanish Toadflax,** Zapitillas, Linaria.

Description: Annual varying in height from about 10 to 25cm; usually only one stem. Leaves narrow, lowest in a whorl, upper alternate. Flowers glandular-hairy or not, varying from white or cream with a light violet spur, to yellow with violet lines, or pinkish. Seeds round, winged.

Flowering: About April to May, June in the hills.

Habitat: Prefers gravelly or stony ground often many growing together.

Distribution: Spain and Portugal; North Africa. Throughout southern Spain; probably most common in hills and mountains.

Family: Linaria family, Scrophulariaceae.

Notes: There are two distinct sub-species in our area, one being hairless, but it is a confusing genus with so many species in Spain. Ripe seeds, which are either winged or not, are necessary for identification.

LINARIA SPARTEA, **Southern Toadflax,** Baleo montesino.

Description: Annual, about 60cm tall with thin erect stems, mainly hairless but some glandular hairs on non-flowering parts and sparse on flowerheads. Leaves linear. Flowers only occasionally violet; slightly scented. Seeds rough, black, unwinged.

Flowering: February to July.

Habitat: Sand, often in crevices amongst rocks in the coarse sand formed from water-worn stone; common in lowlands to mountains.

Distribution: Spain, Portugal, France, possibly North Africa; throughout our area.

Family: Linaria family, Scrophulariaceae.

Notes: Very closely related to another species, L.*viscosa* and not easily separated; the latter is more glandular-hairy especially the flowerheads, basal leaves are wider than the stem leaves, but both vary in these characters.

VERBASCUM PULVERULENTUM, **Hoary Mullein,** Gordolobo.

Description: Tall biennial, to about 1.25m; greyish white hairs. Leaves not lobed but sometimes with small notched margins. Flowers in a much branched head; individual flowers commonly 2-2.5cm across; stamens with white hairs.

Flowering: Early summer, about May to July.

Habitat: Mainly in dry limestone soils, frequent in the east in mountains; rare in southwest of our area.

Distribution: Central and southern Europe.

Family: Linaria family, Scrophulariaceae.

Notes: There is another species common in central and northern Spain with similar candelabra-like heads. It is V. *lychnitis,* and has white or yellow flowers and leaves which clasp the stem (decurrent). It is mainly north of our area, but may reach some high southern mountains.

***ACANTHUS MOLLIS*, Bear's Breeches,** Acanto, Alas de angel.

Description: Strong growing perennial herb, dying back in summer. Leaves deeply lobed, mostly basal and large, 20x40cm or more, on long stalks. Flowers in tall narrow heads a metre or more high, each flower about 4-6cm long, white with purple markings.

Flowering: March to May, June in hills.

Habitat: Abundant on dry limestone on hillsides but usually in some shade; on non-limestone in damp shaded places, often near streams. Lowlands to mountains.

Distribution: West and central Mediterranean area; abundant on Gibraltar, rather rare in nearby Spain, except on calcareous outcrops; commonly cultivated.

Family: Fittonia and Justicia family, Acanthaceae.

Notes: The leaves from this plant were patterns for the design on capitals of many Corinthian pillars of the ancient world.

***OROBANCHE HAENSELERI*, Broomrape,** Rabo de lobo.

Description: Erect parasitic plant with no green leaves. Reddish-brown stems, glandular-hairy; flowers dull orange-red, upper lip deeply lobed. Parasitic on *Helleborous foetidus*.

Flowering: May to early July.

Habitat: Rocky slopes of mountains behind Costa del Sol, usually above 900m, locally common.

Distribution: Endemic to this area of southern Spain.

Family: Broomrape family, Orobanchaceae.

Notes: There are many species of Broomrape in southern Spain, several parasitic on members of the pea family.   Green leaves and flowers in the foreground belong to the host plant, *Helleborous*.

***PLANTAGO LAGOPUS*, Mediterranean Plantain,** Lengua de perro.

Description: Small herb, not woody; perennial, occasionally annual. Leaves in basal rosettes, sometimes on the stem, long - pointed at both ends and widest near the middle of the leaf; veins straight, parallel; leaf mid-green about 10-13x 2-3cm. Flowers in heads on long stems about 18-25cm., many tiny flowers together in rather short elongated heads (compared with other species); calyx has fine shaggy hairs on it; heads remain after flowers are finished.

Flowering: March to June or July.

Habitat: Open places, semi-shade, sandy or loose soil; edges of woods, grassy fields, roadsides, common.

Distribution: Southern Europe.

Family: Plantain, Plantaginaceae.

Notes: There are about a dozen species from lowlands to high mountains here and some species are difficult to separate; the hairs on the calyx (use lens) and the comparatively short head helps to identify this species.

LONICERA ARBOREA, **Tree Honeysuckle,** Cerecillo.

Description: Wide and bushy small tree to about 8m, but sometimes remaining as a small shrub a metre or so high. Leaves variable in shape, about 4-5cm long with very short stalks, usually softly hairy underneath. Flowers in an almost stalkless bunch, scentless except at night. Berries creamy-yellow.

Flowering: June to August.

Habitat: Amongst rocks in mountains, usually steep ground where there is good drainage.

Distribution: Southern Spain, North Africa; in our area, eastwards from Ronda mountains, over 1,000m.

Family: Elder and Guelder Rose family, Caprifoliaceae.

Notes: There is another similar species, L. *xylosteum* in a similar habitat in southern Spain; leaves are larger, but also variable in size and shape; flowers dark cream and berries bright red. The common climbing Honeysuckles are mostly called Madreselva in Spain.

***FEDIA CORNUCOPIAE,* Fedia,** Lechuguilla de la Alcarria.

Description: Small, low-growing and spreading annual; leaves rather dark green and hairless, almost fleshy. Flowers on stems with leaf-like bracts which are toothed; each flower less than 2cm long, tubular with a small pouch at the base; upper part of stems swollen in fruit.

Flowering: December to April.

Habitat: Grassy roadsides, damp pastures and disturbed ground.

Distribution: Mediterranean area, Portugal, North Africa. Widespread in southern Spain.

Family: Valerian family, Valerianaceae.

Notes: There are two species recognised in our area, but are difficult to distinguish in the fields. *Fedia* is a good butterfly and bee plant.

DIPSACUS FULLONUM, **Common or Fuller's Teasel,** Carda, Cardencha.

Description: Robust and prickly perennial herb growing to over a metre; stems erect with short triangular prickles on angles. Leaves stalkless, opposite, lower sharply toothed, upper less so or without any. Flowers very small pinkish or lilac in a large green head.

Flowering: June to August.

Habitat: Damp grassy meadows, roadside ditches, amongst shrubs in light woods but always in damp ground.

Distribution: Most of Europe, North Africa; widespread in our area.

Family: Devil's Bit or Scabious family, Dipsacaceae.

Notes: The dried head is used for raising nap on cloth and for combing wool for which the verb *card* was used. It comes from the Latin *Carduus* meaning a thistle. The Teasel is native here, but another very similar species, D. *sativus*, is cultivated, possibly north of our area; its origin is unknown.

CAMPANULA MOLLIS, **Southern Campanula,** Campanillas.

Description: Low growing perennial with short stems, hanging or erect. Leaves stalkless, wide, greyish with soft hairs. Flowers about 1.5-2cm across, blue to almost lilac.

Flowering: May to July.

Habitat: Prefers cliffs or steep banksides on limestone rocks; in shelter or in open places on roadsides. Mid altitudes to mountains; common.

Distribution: Confined to southern Spain, from southwest to east in our area.

Family: Bell-flower family, Campanulaceae.

Notes: An attractive species forming loose mats. Recent botanical work in Spain shows that this plant should be called C. *velutina,* which is an old name.

CAMPANULA SPECULARIOIDES, **Campanula,** Campanillas.

Description: Spreading hairless annual; stems slender, not more than 20cm high but much branched and often flat, forming open patches. Leaves oval, pointed or blunt, almost without stalks, and few when in flower. Flowers deep lilac to almost magenta, each about 1cm across.

Flowering: June to July.

Habitat: In open rocky places, rough sloping ground and dry cliffs; frequent.

Distribution: Southern Spain in mountains from about Grazalema eastwards.

Family: Bell-flower family, Campanulaceae.

Notes: Named because of its similarity to the flowers of Venus' Looking-glass which used to be called *Specularia.*

TRACHELIUM CAERULEUM, **Throatwort,** Flor de viuda, Hermosilla.

Description: Perennial herb with a thinnish flower-stalk commonly 25-75cm long. Leaves on the stalks variable in shape from wide to fairly narrow, margins with teeth of two lengths (like a saw). Flowers in flat to rounded heads, blue-lilac through to almost pink, occasionally white; each flower with a long slender tube and a stamen protruding for about the same length.

Flowering: June to September, but in damp shaded places often until November.

Habitat: Walls, rock crevices or in damp places above streams, shaded or in sun especially in limestone areas.

Distribution: Western Mediterranean - Spain, Sicily, Portugal and naturalised in France. Lowlands to mountains.

Family: Bell-flower family, Campanulaceae.

Notes: Conspicuous on roadside banks and rock walls, especially in Gibraltar where it grows in crevices in cement and stone walls amongst the town buildings and often together with the Snapdragon (*Anterrhinum barrelieri*).

ANACYCLUS RADIATUS, **Yellow Daisy,** Albijar.

Description: Annual herb 20-80cm high, branched with comparatively thick stems, often pink, covered with very short matted hairs, stem widening below the flowerhead. Flowerheads 4-6cm across; in some plants the flowers are reddish-purple beneath; the green involucral bracts are oblong, the inner each capped by a large dry appendage with a fringed edge. Fruit dry achenes, the outer winged with large sharp-pointed lobes (use lens); inner very narrowly winged.

Flowering: April to July.

Habitat: Open grassy and stony fields, waste places, common.

Distribution: Mediterranean region, Portugal, North Africa.

Family: Daisy family, Compositae (Asteraceae).

Notes: The plants with the flowers that are purplish below seem to be later in flowering than the all-yellow ones. Another species also very common here is A. *clavatus* with white flowers; stems are also thick and swollen below the flowerhead; involucral bracts are usually lanceolate without an appendage but have a narrow purplish or white dry margin; achenes have rounded lobes.

ANDRYALA INTEGRIFOLIA, **Rabbits' Bread,** Pan de Conejo, Carmelita descalza.

Description: Variable herb usually less than a metre high; annual or biennial sometimes flowering a third year; nearly all parts softly hairy with star-shaped and simple hairs and sometimes a few glandular hairs. Leaves soft in texture, narrow, commonly about 7cm long x 3cm wide. Flowerheads pale yellow, about 1.5cm wide, each on thin branched stems; buds covered with buff hairs.

Flowering: April to June or early July.

Habitat: Open places in soft rubble and sand, also in rocky places in light soil. Very common.

Distribution: Mediterranean Europe, Portugal, in southern Spain from the coast into the hills.

Family: Daisy family, Compositae (Asteraceae).

Notes: Distinguished by the whole plant being soft to the touch. It often grows in masses on roadsides in late spring. Whether the Spanish name of Rabbits' Bread refers to the food of rabbits (yet plants do not seem to be damaged in this way), or merely that it is as soft as a rabbit and thus suitable as food I do not know. There are several other species of *Andryala* in our area which are rather similar.

ARCTOTHECA CALENDULA, **Cape Weed.**

Description: Annual, almost fleshy with mealy flowering stems not more than 25-30cm tall. Leaves in flat rosettes but a few from the base of the flowering stem slightly ascending; grey-green and slightly rough, white woolly below. Flowerheads solitary, about 5cm across, purplish underneath. Achenes densely white woolly.

Flowering: February or March to June.

Habitat: Locally abundant in coastal brackish sands, waste places, sandy roadsides; flat land never far from the sea.

Distribution: South Africa, naturalised in southwest Spain, Portugal, spreading.

Family: Daisy family, Compositae (Asteraceae).

Notes: This plant has been naturalised in the Doñana National Park, at Tarifa and Bolonia near Algeciras, and is spreading fast. Previously called *Cryptostemma calendulacea.*

ASTERISCUS MARITIMUS, **Sea Daisy,** Chuchera.

Description: Low growing, bushy perennial usually not more than 50cm high, often less; rough to the touch (scabrid). Leaves rather narrow with entire margins; the green involucral bracts are longer than the buds but at maturity the flowering part exceeds them (seen in the plate). Flowerheads 4-6cm across.

Flowering: March to July, but usually have a few flowers most of the year.

Habitat: Coastal; on steep banks, rock cliffs within the zone of salt-laden winds.

Distribution: Mainly west Mediterranean, Portugal; all coastal southern Spain.

Family: Daisy family, Compositae (Asteraceae).

Notes: A conspicuous plant when in flower. Another species, A. *aquaticus* is small with soft leaves and the involucre is longer than the small flowering head. Grows in meadows and seasonally damp places.

***BELLIS ANNUA,* Annual Daisy,** Margaridoya.

Description: Small annual variable in shape and size but usually less than 15cm high; spreading with several stems. Leaves pale, hairy or almost hairless, variable in shape. Flowers on slender erect stems which may be leafy, flowerheads about 2cm wide, white or occasionally pale lilac. Achenes pubescent.

Flowering: December to May.

Habitat: In sand, grassy fields, in light seasonally damp soils, often near the sea.

Distribution: Mediterranean area, Portugal, North Africa. In southern Spain common in lowlands and hills.

Family: Daisy family, Compositae (Asteraceae).

Notes: The only annual *Bellis* in this area. Those with lilac flowers are rare here and are usually in sandy saline soils, but in Morocco it is the common form.

***BELLIS PERENNIS*, Daisy,** Maya, Pascueta, Bellorita.

Description: Small perennial herb with erect flowering stems to about 15 or 20cm. Leaves all basal, variable in shape and size; blade usually abruptly narrowed to the stalk. Flowerheads about 3-4cm across and sometimes pink beneath. Achenes pubescent.

Flowering: Commonly February to April.

Habitat: In the hills in damp meadows, edges of woods and in higher altitudes, amongst mossy rocks.

Distribution: Widespread in Europe; usually above 300m in southern Spain.

Family: Daisy family, Compositae (Asteraceae).

Notes: Replaced in the lowlands of our area by a similar species (*Bellis sylvestris* p.169) which has leaves with 3 distinct veins, more or less parallel. B. *perennis* has one central vein and thin side veins branching from it. *Bellis* species tend to hybridise if growing near each other.

BELLIS SYLVESTRIS, **Common Daisy,** Margarita.

Description: Small perennial herb with slightly fleshy roots. Leaves variable in shape, 3 veined (1 central long vein, 2 shorter from base); about 3-4cm at widest part; margins shallowly notched or entire, and gradually tapered to the stalk. Flowers on thin erect stalks commonly between 10-25cm long; flowerheads variable in width but usually about 4cm across; ligules sometimes purplish-pink underneath but more commonly white.

Flowering: November to June, main flowering between February and April.

Habitat: Very common on edges of woods, roadsides, grassy fields; often in seasonally damp places in shade or sun.

Distribution: Southern Europe.

Family: Daisy family, Compositae (Asteraceae).

Notes: There are 4 species in our area, and B. *rotundifolia,* confined to the southwest, is the largest with a rounded leaf abruptly contracted to the stalk; flowerheads may be 4-5cm wide.

CALENDULA SUFFRUTICOSA, **Rock Marigold,** Caléndula.

Description: Perennial with spreading stems 25-30cm high. Leaves alternate on stems usually stalkless; margins entire to variously notched. Flowerheads 3-6cm across. Fruit, outer achenes curved and thin and long-beaked, hairless or with a few glands.

Flowering: March to May, June in the hills.

Habitat: Rocky ground on coastal cliffs or in dry ground; on hills, mainly in limestone in crevices or stony ground at cliff bases.

Distribution: Spain and Portugal.

Family: Daisy family, Compositae (Asteraceae).

Notes: There are 3 sub-species in our area: ssp. *tomentosa* is distinct with white, woolly hairs on the stems and leaves; it is common in the southwest. The garden Marigold is commonly cultivated, sometimes becoming naturalised. The Field Marigold, C. *arvensis,* an annual with tiny flowers, is very common throughout our area.

CENTAUREA PULLATA ssp. pullata, **Southern Knapweed,** Centaurea.

Description: Low-growing perennial or biennial variable in habit but usually low-growing to about 40cm high; nearly all parts hairy. Leaves mid-green, the basal ones lobed with the largest at the apex; upper leaves clasping the stem, lobed or entire and there is always a "collar" of comparatively narrow leaf-like bracts at the base of the flowerhead. Flowers in a head of about 4-5cm across on the top of a capitulum which is almost round, pinched in at the top and covered with overlapping green scales edged with black, the apex of each with pale soft spines shaped like a fan; the uppermost row of bracts is spineless and edged with black.

Flowering: February to May or June.

Habitat: Grassy and bushy places, rough ground, roadsides and sandy soil.

Distribution: Spain, Portugal, North Africa. Common in southern Spain, but the newly described sub-species *baetica*, an annual, is perhaps more common in the southwest.

Family: Daisy family, Compositae (Asteraceae).

Notes: There are over 200 species of *Centaurea* in Europe, many of them in Spain; C. *pullata* is distinguished from other southern Spanish species by its leafy collar and spineless capitula.

171

CHAMAEMELUM FUSCATUM, **Marsh Chamomile,** Margarza.

Description: Annual herb, soft and hairless, no higher than 30cm. Leaves divided into very finely cut sharp-pointed segments, dark green. Flowers in heads each about 2-3cm across; involucral bracts egg-shaped, each with a dark brown margin. Fruit, dry achenes about 1mm long, slightly ridged, not winged. Plants have a strong, not very pleasant smell.

Flowering: December to April, but May to June if season is wet and cool; fades rapidly in heat and dry ground.

Habitat: Seasonally flooded and low-lying fields, marshes, roadside ditches; usually in flat land, mainly open places in lowlands; often in great masses covering fields with white.

Distribution: Western Mediterranean area to northwest Spain, Portugal, North Africa.

Family: Daisy family, Compositae (Asteraceae).

Notes: Distinguished by its habitat and early flowering, but there are many other white-flowered daisies in our area, and all are difficult to identify without seed and a hand lens.

CHRYSANTHEMUM CORONARIUM, **Crown Daisy,** Ojo de buey, Mirabeles.

Description: Rather strong-growing annual with tough stems, 20-90cm high. Leaves stalkless cut into oblong, deeply toothed segments. Flowers large, 4-6cm across, either all lemon-yellow, or white with orange-yellow at the base; outer involucral bracts egg-shaped with a brown band behind the whitish dry margin, inner bracts with a wide dry margin only, but with a pale appendage at the apex. Fruit, inner achenes with an angled wing on one side and ribbed on the face; outer 3 angled with wings.

Flowering: March to June.

Habitat: Open places; fields, uncultivated land, roadsides; both colours common; coastal to hills.

Distribution: Mediterranean, Portugal, sometimes in other parts of Europe as escapes from cultivation.

Family: Daisy family, Compositae (Asteraceae).

Notes: A more easily distinguished daisy than the white ones. The first Spanish name means Ox-eye.

DITTRICHIA VISCOSA, **Sticky Inula,** Altabaca, Matamosquitos.

Description:　Bushy perennial with many erect stems; about 50-150cm high, most parts with short but sticky glandular hairs; stems pale green. Leaves stemless, alternate, clasping the main-stems; pointed and with a wavy margin. Flowerheads about 1.50cm across opening in succession over a long period, so spent and new heads are mixed.

Flowering:　July to November.

Habitat:　Dry stony places, road verges, scrubland and light pinewoods, common; coastal to hills.

Distribution:　Southern and eastern Spain, Portugal, southern France. Abundant in our area.

Family:　Daisy, Compositae (Asteraceae).

Notes:　Conspicuous when in flower especially in the countryside when little else is out. In earlier books it is called *Inula viscosa* and the two differ in the following:　Achenes not contracted below pappus, pappus hairs free = *Inula.* Achenes abruptly contracted below the pappus, pappus hairs joined at the base = *Dittrichia* (use lens).

DORONICUM PLANTAGINEUM, **Leopard's Bane.**

Description: Perennial with flowering stems to 70cm. Leaves basal narrowed into a long stalk; stem leaves stalkless and wide at the base, clasping the stem then narrowing to a pointed apex; an occasional narrow upper leaf. Flowerhead normally solitary, about 5cm across on rather thin erect stems, glandular-hairy.

Flowering: April to July (August, Sierra Nevada).

Habitat: Frequent in mountains from about 1,000m to sub-alpine pastures, usually in shade of woods and damp, sheltered places.

Distribution: Western Europe; Spain; Portugal, France and Italy; cultivated elsewhere, sometimes naturalised.

Family: Daisy family, Compositae (Asteraceae).

Notes: A distinctive mountain species usually growing in clumps. There are about 5 other species in Spain, but only this one is in our area. *Doronicum* leaves were used dried for snuff centuries ago.

HELICHRYSUM STOECHAS, **Everlasting, Curry Plant,** Pepétuas silvestre.

Description: Woody perennial commonly about 50-75cm high with erect or spreading aromatic branches, white woolly. Leaves white to green above, white beneath, leaf-margins rolled under. Flowers, each flowerhead about 5-6mm across, many of these forming a loose secondary head (corymb); the actual flower is very small and hidden by overlapping shiny membraneous bracts which are yellow, never green.

Flowering: April to August, September in the mountains.

Habitat: In sand and rocky places, frequently on limestone but also on other rough, uncultivated places throughout our area.

Distribution: Most of southern Europe, North Africa; this and other similar species widely cultivated elsewhere.

Family: Daisy family, Compositae (Asteraceae).

Notes: The shiny yellow bracts remain after flowering which makes it a good garden plant and some cultivars are strongly aromatic and have the smell of a poor curry. It has been used in folk medicine since at least the first century A.D.

LEUZEA CONIFERA, **Pine-cone Knapweed,** Piña de San Juan.

Description: Short perennial herb, occasionally dying after flowering; not more than 25-30cm high; stems felted, pale, usually leafy. Leaves with white felted hairs below and margins often with long lobes. Flowers with green to cherry-red, erect stems, corolla from pink to almost white from the top of the pale chaff-like bracts.

Flowering: June to August.

Habitat: Dry heathlands amongst shrubs in rocky ground or sand in light woods; from lowlands to mountains, locally common.

Distribution: West Mediterranean area, Portugal.

Family: Daisy family, Compositae (Asteraceae).

Notes: An unusual plant but conspicuous with its bracts (involucre) which look like a miniature pine-cone and last long after the flowers have finished. In some books it is called *Centaurea conifera.*

REICHARDIA GADITANA, **Sand Reichardia,** Lechuguilla dulce.

Description: Low and spreading biennial or perennial, occasionally annual. Leaves variable, blue-green with slightly to deeply toothed margins. Flowers in heads, 3-4cm across with overlapping yellow ligules and brown bases; involucral bracts in several rows with pale margins. Fruits (achenes) wrinkled horizontally.

Flowering: February to June.

Habitat: Mainly on coastal sands at back of beaches where it forms patches.

Distribution: Southern Spain, Portugal, North Africa.

Family: Daisy family, Compositae (Asteraceae).

Notes: Once very common, now only on undisturbed areas of beaches, often with the pink flowered *Malcolmia* and *Matthiola* species. Superficially it resembles Tolpis (see page180). The name *gaditana* comes from the latin for Cadiz (Gades), the ancient town which was built by the Phoenicians.

SCORZONERA CRISPATULA, **Viper's Grass,** Escorzonera.

Description: Tuberous perennial; most parts with very fine cobwebby hairs. Leaves, lowest to 25cm long; margins wavy to crisped, lobes with thin teeth. Flowers about 5 or 6cm across; the green involucral bracts shorter than the ligules (see *Tragopogon* p.181); some plants are all yellow without the dark centre.

Flowering: April to July.

Habitat: Dry rocky and rough ground, open places, usually inland and in the hills.

Distribution: Southern and eastern Spain, southern France, Portugal. More frequent in central and eastern area of southern Spain.

Family: Daisy family, Compositae (Asteraceae).

Notes: Very closely related to the vegetable Scorzonera (S. *hispanica*) and considered in some publications to be only a variety of it. The vegetable comes from a taller plant with larger leaves (to 40cm long) and flowers usually without any dark centre.

TOLPIS BARBATA, Tolpis.

Description: Slender annual occasionally biennial (see Notes below); variable in shape and size, usually with many interlacing thin branchlets and spreading, not much more than 30cm high. Leaves rather pale green, margins usually with sharp-pointed shallow lobes. Flowers with green erect bracts much longer than the bud; flowers to about 5cm across with a pale centre at first but maturing to a dark chocolate colour; bracts conspicuous when in seed.

Flowering: April to June.

Habitat: Open places, dry, sandy or grassy ground, rubble and roadside gravel, usually in the lowlands, especially coastal areas; less common in the hills.

Distribution: Southern Europe, North Africa.

Family: Daisy family, Compositae (Asteraceae).

Notes: The plate of Tolpis is probably an annual form of what used to be called var. *grandiflora*. There are three species now recognised in our area and they possibly hybridise. One other plant could be mistaken for the dark-eyed Tolpis; it is the annual *Hispidella*, usually north of this area. The leaf margins are entire and there are brownish-yellow ligules surrounding the dark centre and shorter than the outer yellow ones. Also compare with *Reichardia* (p.178).

TRAGOPOGON PORRIFOLIUS, **Salsify, Oyster Plant,** Barba cabruna, Barbón común.

Description: Soft herb, biennial or occasionally annual, about half a metre tall, often less; root tuberous, pale. Leaves long, narrow but widened at the base, rather pale blue-green and soft. Flower stem erect and noticeably swollen below the solitary flowerhead; the green bracts always longer than the purple part, the whole being about 6-8cm across. Seedhead conspicuous, buff with fine feathery hairs crowning the achenes.

Flowering: March to May.

Habitat: Grassy and cultivated fields, country roadsides, thickets and edges of woods, usually in light soils; throughout our area.

Distribution: Mediterranean Europe, Portugal, North Africa, but often naturalised in other countries through cultivation.

Family: Daisy family, Compositae (Asteraceae).

Notes: Has been cultivated for centuries as a vegetable. The fleshy taproot looking like a poor-quality parsnip has an oyster flavour when cooked and now good cultivars with thick tubers are grown world-wide but not much used in Spanish cooking. An older name is Vegetable Oyster.

CARLINA RACEMOSA, **Clustered Carline Thistle,** Cardo de la uva.

Description: Very spiny and stiffly branched annual, occasionally persisting for a further year or two. Seldom more than 40cm tall, usually less; stems and young leaves with fine white, woolly hairs. Leaves pale green, narrow and folded; margins with hard and very sharp spines at intervals. Flowers in compound heads surrounded by yellow petal-like bracts about 3cm across.

Flowering: July to October.

Habitat: Dry and stony places, uncultivated ground and often with Ragwort; abundant.

Distribution: Southern Spain, Portugal, Italy (Sardinia), North Africa.

Family: Thistle and Daisy family, Compositae (Asteraceae).

Notes: Even when the flowers are finished, the tough yellow bracts remain bright. When the plant dies it stays intact for some months, which makes for unpleasant walking through land where this ankle-biter grows.

CARTHAMUS ARBORESCENS, **Yellow Woody Thistle,** Cardo cabrero.

Description: Branched but open woody shrub to over 2m tall. Leaves glandular hairy, most of them deeply lobed and with pale spines. Flowerheads large, about 3.5-6cm wide.

Flowering: May to July.

Habitat: In hot and dry places especially in hills, mainly on limestone, roadsides and steep rocky banks.

Distribution: Endemic to south - southeast Spain; rare in southwest except for Gibraltar (on the steep limestone cliffs).

Family: Thistle and Daisy family, Compositae (Asteraceae).

Notes: A large thistle conspicuous with its huge yellow flowerheads and pale leaves. It has a strong unpleasant smell of goats.

CHAMAELEON GUMMIFER, **Stemless Thistle,** Ajonjera.

Description: Flat, stemless perennial with thick underground tubers which spread from the parent plant, so that there are often several plants together. Leaves in an open rosette are spiny and lobed almost to the midrib, commonly 30x12cm long; usually dead at flowering time. Flowers stemless in centre of rosette with cobwebby hairs on the involucre; heads pink, occasionally white, about 6cm across.

Flowering: From about August to November.

Habitat: Open dry and grassy fields and hillsides in heavy soils.

Distribution: Mediterranean area, Portugal. In southern Spain lowlands to hills.

Family: Thistle and Daisy family, Compositae (Asteraceae).

Notes: It seems strange to see a healthy pink flower in the midst of a presumably dead plant. When the flower dies it blows away in autumn winds, dispersing its seeds well away from the parent plant. Previously known as *Atractylis gummifera*.

***CIRSIUM ECHINATUM,* Hill Thistle,** Cardo de arrecife.

Description: Perennial, low and spreading branches. Leaves sparsely to densely covered with white cobwebby hairs; lobes with long golden spines. Flowers on short stalks; involucre also hairy with strong yellow spines.

Flowering: June to August.

Habitat: Stony and rubbly ground in open country, paths and mountainsides, often in seasonally damp ground; about 650m to high altitudes.

Distribution: Western Mediterranean area; common in the mountains behind the coast.

Family: Thistle and Daisy family, Compositae (Asteraceae).

Notes: There are many attractive thistles in Spain and, as most are difficult to identify, rather a lot have been included.

***CIRSIUM SCABRUM*, Giant Thistle,** Cardo alto.

Description: Biennial or sometimes not flowering until the third year; very tall, erect about 2-3m in height, one long stem branched above. Leaves first year very large, deeply cut into wide lobes with spiny tips; white-woolly beneath. Flowers pink in relatively small heads 1-3 together; stem and branches white.

Flowering: May to July.

Habitat: Open countryside, grassy fields and edges of country roadsides, light woods, mainly damp places and frequently above streams; less common in rubbly dry ground.

Distribution: Western Mediterranean region, North Africa; in southern Spain from lowlands to mid mountains.

Family: Thistle and Daisy family, Compositae (Asteraceae).

Notes: Our tallest thistle and thus easy to identify. It is called C. *giganteum* in some books, more apropos!

GALACTITES TOMENTOSA, **Thistle,** Cardo común.

Description: Annual thistle with erect stems to 100cm but often less. Leaves at first in a striking rosette of green and white flat leaves, with fine yellow spines on margins and a white felting underneath. Flowers on leafy white stems which are winged to about half-way up; flowerheads stalked, one to several at the top of the stem.

Flowering: March to June.

Habitat: Fields, roadsides and waste ground, abundant.

Distribution: Mediterranean region, Portugal, North Africa. Widely spread in southern Spain from coasts to mountains.

Family: Thistle and Daisy family, Compositae (Asteraceae).

Notes: Probably our most common thistle, covering the countryside with the purplish-pink flowers. In the southeast there is another similar species (G. *duriaei*) which appears to differ in having rather longer and stouter spines and the flowerheads are almost stalkless.

PTILOSTEMON HISPANICUS, **Spanish Mountain Thistle.**

Description: Perennial but often short-lived; low and compact when young with conspicuous rosettes mainly of golden spines. Leaves deep green, shiny above, white below and liberally armed with long and short formidable prickles of a deep yellow. Flowers several, terminal on long white and leafy stalks which may reach 100cm.

Flowering: June or July to November.

Habitat: Open places in limestone crevices, rubble and sand in the windswept high altitudes from about 400m upwards.

Distribution: Endemic to southern Spain, frequent throughout our area except in the southwest.

Family: Thistle and Daisy family, Compositae (Asteraceae).

Notes: One of the most attractive of the pink-flowering thistles here. Easily distinguished by the shiny dark green leaves and golden spines. An older name is *Chamaepeuce.*

SCOLYMUS HISPANICUS, **Spanish Thistle, Oyster Plant,** Tagarnina.

Description: Spiny biennial or perennial dying down in late summer; most of the plant has very sharp and hard, pale spines and mainly one tall stem to 1.50 or 2m with many shorter side branches. Leaves deeply or shallowly lobed, stalkless and clasping the stems. Flowerheads 4-5cm wide when fully open, many; basal branches often with terminal flowerheads as well.

Flowering: May to July.

Habitat: Dry open places in neutral or acid soils, abundant in fields, roadsides etc. Less common on limestone.

Distribution: Widespread in southern Europe, coastal and lowlands; North Africa. Common in Spain to about 900m in the southeast.

Family: Daisy family, Compositae (Asteraceae).

Notes: A famous food-plant of the southwest. At the first autumn rains Tagarnina appears as a flat rosette of dark spiny leaves. These are cut, the leafy part removed, leaving a pale midrib which is used in stews and omelettes. The latter, Tortilla de Tagarnina, is excellent and is served in most roadside ventas. There is a similar species, an annual, no more than 1m tall and with a strongly winged stem. It has no rosette and does not appear to be eaten.

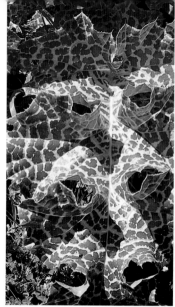

***SILYBUM MARIANUM*, Milk Thistle,** Lechero.

Description: Large-leaved perennial, occasionally annual. Leaves shiny, mottled; basal very large, lobed not flat, upper smaller. Flowering stems to 2m, erect and leafy; flowerheads pink 4-5cm wide surrounded by stiff sharp spines.

Flowering: April to June.

Habitat: Open places in waste, disturbed and seasonally damp ground especially on short banks.

Distribution: Widespread in the Mediterranean and southeast Europe, abundant in southern Spain, cultivated elsewhere; North Africa.

Family: Daisy family, Compositae (Asteraceae).

Notes: Used medicinally in the past. Gerard's Herbal, (16 cent.) states that the plant is excellent against melancholy. Young leaves and midribs are edible. It is sometimes confused in literature with the Holy or Blessed Thistle, *Cnicus benedictus*, which has yellow flowers and is an annual.

ALLIUM AMPELOPRASUM, **Wild Leek,** Puerro silvestre.

Description: Bulb about 4-8cm diameter with small bulbils at base; stems erect, stout from about 50cm to over 1m high. Leaves several, with rough margins, withering as flowers appear. Flowerheads commonly 7-9cm diameter, comprising many tiny flowers, commonly pink but also almost purplish or white; one papery spathe falling when flowers appear.

Flowering: April to early July.

Habitat: Open fields, rough and cultivated, roadsides, heathlands, often in large patches; common in our area from coast to hills.

Distribution: Southern and western Europe; North Africa.

Family: Lily family, Liliaceae.

Notes: ˙ A variable plant. Possibly a parent of the cultivated leek.

ALLIUM NIGRUM, Giant Onion.

Description: Bulb about 4cm across; stem erect to 1m. Leaves large about 50 x 7cm, usually 3-4; almost flat and wide at the base tapering to a pointed apex; strong garlic smell. Flowerhead on a bare round stalk, hairless and tough in texture; flowers white or pink, many to a head with a large spathe subtending the head, splitting as it matures into several segments shorter than the width of the flowerhead; flowers with a honeysuckle scent.

Flowering: April to June.

Habitat: Cultivated fields, seasonally damp ground often in heavy clay, roadsides; coastal to about 1,000m.

Distribution: Much of the Mediterranean area, Portugal.

Family: Lily family, Liliaceae.

Notes: One of our largest Alliums and in some areas pink flowers predominate, in others the white, but are less commonly mixed.

ASPHODELUS ALBUS, **Asphodel,** Gamon.

Description: Perennial herb with tuberous roots and one erect stem to about a metre and often a few short side branches from the lower part of stem. Leaves basal, long, about 60 x 1-2cm, pointed and rather light green. Flowers with dark brown bracts and brown lines on buds and less so on flowers. Fruit an almost round capsule, 1.5-2cm, light brown.

Flowering: March to June.

Habitat: Seasonally damp places in grassy fields, in light woods and mossy meadows; commonest in hills and mountains.

Distribution: Southern Europe, North Africa.

Family: Lily family, Liliaceae.

Notes: There are two other species (and a small biennial of sandy soil, A. *fistulosus*) in our area. A. *aestivus*, which is abundant in open uncultivated fields covering them with white in spring, is mainly a lowland species. It has several branched stems, pale bracts and small oblong fruits widest at the apex and less than 1cm across. The other species is not so easily distinguished; it is A. *ramosa*, which has side branches often as long as the main one. Capsules are round, but only about 1cm wide. It is common in both lowlands and hills.

COLCHICUM LUSITANUM, **Southern Colchicum,** Cólchico.

Description: Leafless when in flower, but wide and shiny leaves with wavy margins appear in early spring and grow to about 25cm. Flowers solitary or in clusters of six or more, each appearing from a separate corm, which have black, shiny jackets. Flowers from pale to mid-pink with white, giving a checkered pattern Large seed capsules develop with the leaves. (See also *Crocus*, p.206).

Flowering: September to early November.

Habitat: In dry open fields, in hard ground and where cattle graze, in rocky and limestone places (conspicuous in Gibraltar) from the coast to the hills. Throughout southern Spain.

Distribution: Spain, especially the Mediterranean area, Italy and Portugal.

Family: Lily family, Liliaceae.

Notes: Being leafless, flowers are fed by the corm, an adaption to flowering in drought. Heavy rain often rots the flowers. Corms contain the drug colchicum, which has been used for centuries in treating rheumatism and gout.   Corms are frequently eaten by the White Toothed Shrew, which lives, apparently symbolically, in the Blind Moles' burrows.

FRITILLARIA HISPANICA**, Fritillary, Snake's Head,** Meleagria.

Description: Similar to F. *lusitanica* (p.196), but differs in the wider leaves which are opposite each other at the base of the stem; the style is shorter between the stigma and the ovaries, but these differences are not always obvious. The flower is often darker in colour, almost reddish-brown.

Flowering: March to May.

Habitat: More or less as F. *lusitanica,* but reaches sub-alpine in the high Iberian mountains of the south.

Distribution: Widespread in the Mediterranean region.

Family: Lily family, Liliaceae.

Notes: Plants seem to be more common inland, reaching into the higher mountains. The photograph was taken in the Sierra Nevada at over 3,000m amongst the lilac broom (*Erinacea*, p.57) and the spiny *Vella* in the foreground. This is part of the so-called "Hedgehog Zone" comprising spiny, windswept plants of these high Iberian mountains.

FRITILLARIA LUSITANICA, **Fritillary, Snake's Head,** Meleagria.

Description:　Slender bulbous plant, hairless with erect grey stem. Leaves greyish-green, narrow, about 6 to 9cm long and alternate. Flowers commonly one but up to three on a stem, variable in colour and markings, slightly checkered (tessellated) on the outside or not. Capsule erect.

Flowering:　February to May, but to June in the hills.

Habitat:　Often near the coast amongst short growth and with Tulips and Irises; in sandy or dry and heavy soil, from coast to hills.

Distribution:　Spain, southern Portugal, throughout our area.

Family:　Lily family, Liliaceae.

Notes:　Easily spotted when growing in short growth in sandy soil, but elsewhere rather hidden amongst *Cistus* and gorse bushes and then easily missed. There are only two species in southern Spain and they are not always easy to distinguish.

SCILLA PERUVIANA, **Giant Squill,** Albarrana.

Description: Bulb large, leaves basal spreading or almost erect, broad and smooth, about 6 x 50cm or more. Flowering stems about 50cm, topped by a pyramid of about 100 flowers, pyramid flattening with age. Seeds in pale capsule, angled and black.

Flowering: March to May or June, depending on rain.

Habitat: Open, damp and seasonally muddy ground in grassy fields of heavy soil; not limestone.

Distribution: Southwest Spain, Italy, Mediterranean islands, Portugal, northwest Africa. In southern Spain not much further east than the Ronda and Grazalema area.

Family: Lily family, Liliaceae.

Notes: One of the largest Scillas and often cultivated in temperate climates. In the wild it depends on sufficient rain with spring warmth to stimulate flowering, but finishes very quickly if subsequent days are hot and dry. Also leaves are channelled above by upturned margins and are able to direct any moisture, even dew, to the roots.

TULIPA SYLVESTRIS ssp. AUSTRALIS, **Southern Wild Tulip,** Tulipan silvestre.

Description: Plant with bulb. Leaves few, pointed, widened at the base and often twisted. Flowering stem thin, erect about 15 to 30cm tall. Flowers nodding in bud, opening about 5cm across; brick-red on the underside.

Flowering: March to April in lowlands, June to July in high altitudes.

Habitat: Grassy and sandy uncultivated land near the sea, and inland amongst heathers and other bushes on rocky slopes and fields; on hills and mountains often with Fritillary.

Distribution: The sub-species is found in much of southern Europe and through southern Spain.

Family: Lily family, Liliaceae.

Notes: An attractive small Tulip which has little variation in its flowers but has a short flowering period fading quickly in heat. As with Fritillary it does not like being trampled upon and so is disappearing from coastal areas.

URGINEA MARITIMA, **Autumn Squill,** Cebolla albarrana, Esquila.

Description: Bulb very large, 10cm or more in diameter. Leaves basal, large, often 60-80cm long and 10cm wide; they are bright green, shiny and pointed, but are absent when the plant is in flower, appearing when the seed is ripe. Flowers white with a brownish vein and in a dense head; each flower about 3cm across and subtended by two bracts of unequal size. Flowerheads first appear in bud as dark brown, spear-like heads on tall, brown unbranched stems out of dry earth. Seed capsules are three-cornered.

Flowering: September to October, occasionally from August.

Habitat: Common in dry, bare fields, rough slopes, less frequently in open corkwoods. Prefers acid or neutral soils.

Distribution: Southern Europe and fairly common in southern Spain, probably more so in the southwest.

Family: Lily family, Liliaceae.

Notes: Distinguished from the spring-flowering Asphodels, which may look similar, by its autumn blooming. Autumn Squill has been in use for medicine since ancient times, but it also contains a harmful glucoside used for rat poison. The huge bulbs are often exposed after heavy rain, but usually continue growing if only a few of its fleshy roots are in the soil. Previously known as *Scilla maritima.*

199

***LEUCOJUM TRICHOPHYLLUM*, Snowflake,** Campanilla de primavera.

Description: Small bulb with erect flowering stems about 10-25cm; lengthening after flowering. Leaves very narrow about 2-3mm wide, present with flowering stems and slightly shorter. Flowers 1-3 occasionally more, drooping, about 2-3cm long.

Flowering: January to May.

Habitat: Nearly always in sand and light soils in grassy fields and in coastal pinewoods; sometimes in deep pockets of the large rocks on edges of corkwoods, in leaf mould; mainly lowlands.

Distribution: Southern Spain, Portugal, North Africa.

Family: Narcissus family, Amaryllidaceae.

Notes: One of the delightful harbingers of spring. Another species in our area is rather similar, but is autumn flowering (L. *autumnale*) and has stems not more than 20cm high, often less. The slightly wider leaves start to appear when the flowers are out or just over.

NARCISSUS BULBOCODIUM, **Hoop Petticoat Daffodil,** Narciso.

Description: Plant with a small bulb and an erect flowering stem. Leaves to about 35cm, usually much less; width 1.5-3mm. Flowers one to a stalk and more or less horizontal; anthers seldom exceeding the funnel.

Flowering: January to May (occasionally from December in southwest).

Habitat: Seasonally damp, rich soil in crevices and mossy ledges on exposed rock outcrops, as well as in woodlands, fields and in sandy soil. Lowlands to mid-mountains.

Distribution: Widespread in Spain, southwest France, North Africa.

Family: Narcissus family, Amaryllidaceae.

Notes: At least two sub-species in our area and in the Doñana National Park; the plants are tall with slightly paler flowers and some green at their bases. It is common in damp, sandy soil in flat places and also in light woods and open marshlands. The white hoop petticoat daffodil, common on rocks and banks mainly in the hills, is N. *cantabricus* and is confined to southern Spain and North Africa. It tends to flower later than the yellow species.

NARCISSUS PAPYRACEUS, **Paper-white Narcissus,** Narciso.

Description: A bulb with a flowering stem commonly 25-35cm long. Leaves 4 to 6 just over 1cm wide, ridged and flattened towards the thin margins, blue-green. Flowers white, strongly scented (pleasant or not according to one's interpretation), stem rather flattened and ridged.

Flowering: Usually from December to early March, but flowers appear from late October or November if there has been prolonged rain.

Habitat: Wet, heavy soils in fields, roadsides and open places; common in southern Spain especially in clay soils.

Distribution: Widespread in Mediterranean countries.

Family: Narcissus family, Amaryllidaceae.

Notes: Covers fields in great masses like dots of snow and in the coldest weather. Fades quickly in heat. A similar species, N. *tazetta,* which is also native has a yellow cup (the corona) and a sweet scent. It flowers later than the Paper-white.

***NARCISSUS SEROTINUS*,** **Small Pheasant's Eye Narcissus,** Narciso.

Description: Slender, small autumn-flowering bulb, often many together; flowering stems and leaves above 15-20cm long. Leaves sometimes present at flowering, but usually appearing later. Flowers on slender stems, commonly with 1-2 flowers but up to 5 on a stem, strongly scented and about 3-4cm across with a very short corona.

Flowering: October to November, but from September if there have been early rains.

Habitat: Uncultivated grassy fields, sand or gravelly light soil near the coast but also in open spaces amongst light woods and heathlands inland.

Distribution: Mediterranean region, Portugal, North Africa, in southern Spain, mainly lowlands.

Family: Narcissus family, Amaryllidaceae.

Notes: The scent is strong but not so pleasant as the better-known Pheasant's Eye, which is north of our area. This plant once covered fields with white flowers, especially in the sandy soils near the coast, but they resent disturbance and have disappeared in most places there. Sometimes found with N. *viridiflorus* (see p.227) and may hybridize to produce yellowish green flowers.

PANCRATIUM MARITIMUM, **Sea Daffodil,** Nardo marino.

Description: Bulbs large, deeply buried. Leaves flat blue-green, about 50cm long or more by 1.5-2cm; dead before flowers appear; flower-stalks stout, green, erect 20-50cm long. Flowers large, very strongly scented and about 8 or 9 on a stalk subtended by two papery bracts; each flower about 9cm across and the narrow outer segments with a pale green stripe below. Seeds large, black and shiny.

Flowering: July to September.

Habitat: In deep sand at back of beaches, on sand dunes, always near the sea.

Distribution: Mediterranean, Portugal, North Africa; common in southern Spain, but disappearing from development.

Family: Narcissus family, Amaryllidaceae.

Notes: A lovely and easily identified plant. Bulbs are often buried up to two metres in the loose sand and when in flower the brown dead leaves lie untidily around the stem bases. New leaves appear towards the end of flowering, remaining green throughout the winter. Flowers are visited by spectacular moths, such as the Hawkmoths and another, called Kew Arches, which has a beautifully coloured caterpillar of brown, black and white.

***STERNBERGIA LUTEA*, Common Sternbergia.**

Description: Bulbs with smooth tunics, about 4cm wide. Leaves wide, about 1.5 x 20-25cm, dark green with a pale central stripe. Leaves either absent at flowering or developed to a few centimetres but grow rapidly as the flower matures. Flowers about 3.5cm across at first, but opening wider.

Flowering: From about September to November.

Habitat: Rocky hillsides usually over 300m; more frequent in crevices on limestone but in dry places grows near moisture. Not native in the southwest of our area.

Distribution: Mediterranean, North Africa; in southern Spain scattered eastwards from about Gaucin.

Family: Narcissus family, Amaryllidaceae.

Notes: An attractive plant, often cultivated; large patches are in gardens of some government buildings in Grazalema. It looks superificially like a yellow Crocus, but leaves are distinctive and somewhat resemble those of another Spanish bulb, *Lapiedra*, with a similar pale stripe, but these are shorter and the flowers are white.

CROCUS SEROTINUS, **Southern Autumn Crocus,** Azafrán del sur.

Description: Small plant with a corm. Leaves narrow about 1.5-3mm wide, rather dark green with a central groove which is pale; leaves usually start to grow during flowering or have developed by then. Flowers usually one, lilac to pink.

Flowering: October to early December.

Habitat: In shade of corkwoods and in scrub up to tops of hills or in open rocky ground about 650-700m.

Distribution: Spain, Portugal, North Africa; common in our area.

Family: Iris family, Iridaceae.

Notes: There are 3 sub-species which differ in the corm covering; in our area the commonest is ssp. *salzamannii* which is the one in the plate above. (See also *Colchicum* p.194). From about 1,000m in the high mountains there is a distinctive species, C. *nevadensis*, with pale flowers, lined with purple veins and the two grow together at about 1,000m. They are related to the crocus producing Saffron (C. *sativus*), a sterile plant cultivated in northern Spain, but its origin is not known.

GYNANDIRIS (IRIS) SISYRINCHIUM, **Barbary Nut,** Mazuca, Patita de burro.

Description: Small Iris-like herb with corm, one to several stems, variable in branching and flower colour; height from about 15-35cm tall, depending on soil. Leaves just over half a centemetre wide, flat, long and arching, fairly pale green. Flowers ranging from very pale lilac to blue-lilac or violet, with or without a yellow patch on the falls; several to a stem.

Flowering: Commonly from February to June, but in sheltered coastal sands from November or December; many plants flowering at the same time.

Habitat: Dry sandy ground, grassy fields, roadsides, flowers opening about 2.30-3pm and abundant in our area, coastal to mid-mountains.

Distribution: Mediterranean region, Portugal, North Africa.

Family: Iris family, Iridaceae.

Notes: Differs from *Iris* by the rootstock being a corm which resembles a bulb but is actually the swollen base of a stem; Irises have a bulb or a tuberous rhizome. Plants are easily missed until early afternoon, then dull, grassy areas are transformed by hundreds of flowers; these last only one day but are replaced daily over a long period.

IRIS FILIFOLIA, **Purple Iris,** Lirio violeta.

Description: Stem erect, thin, from about 30-100cm tall; rhizome a bulb. Leaves thin, drooping, margins rolled. Flowers reddish-purple with a conspicuous yellow blotch on falls.

Flowering: Late March (coastal), April to June.

Habitat: Stony ground in open places, usually sloping; corkwoods in the southwest; sandstone or limestone; locally frequent but scattered throughout.

Distribution: Southern Spain, North Africa.

Family: Iris family, Iridaceae.

Notes: A beautiful species, previously more common, but suffered from being over-collected. Usually flowers later than the similar, but blue, I. *xiphium.*

IRIS PLANIFOLIA, **Wide-leaved Iris,** Lirio.

Description: Small plant commonly 12-20cm tall. Leaves several, wide, 20-25 x 2-3cm with long drawn-out point usually recurved. Flowers solitary, 9-12cm across on short stalks which elongate in seed; flowers pale lilac to deep blue-lilac, sometimes white, but always with yellow on the falls.

Flowering: Mostly during January to March, but also November and December in some years.

Habitat: In sand and low-lying grassy fields often in heavy, seasonally wet soils in the lowlands; in higher altitudes on open sloping ground and in grassy pockets in shingle or stony places, especially in shale.

Distribution: Mediterranean area, Portugal, North Africa; in southern Spain from lowlands to mid-mountains.

Family: Iris family, Iridaceae.

Notes: Distinctive species with its wide leaves and short stem. Often fills fields with colour early in the year, particularly in the farming land between Algeciras and Jerez.

***IRIS XIPHIUM*, Spanish Iris,** Lirio de España.

Description: Tall plant with a bulb and a erect stem up to 80cm, often much less, especially in the hills. Leaves long, very narrow (about 5mm across), green with grey in the centre. Flowers deep rich blue, more than one to a stem. Usually many plants growing together.

Flowering: January to March at sea-level, but to June in mountains.

Habitat: Mainly grassy fields and ditches, wet in winter, also open roadsides and corkwood edges; usually in heavy soil, sea level to mountains.

Distribution: Southwest Mediterranean and Portugal; Morocco.

Family: Iris family, Iridaceae.

Notes: A gregarious species covering damp fields with blue, but alas, eagerly picked. In the extreme southwest of our area is a form with pale lilac-blue flowers which appear in April. It has been called I. *tingitana*, which is a Moroccan species and grows in sandy soil in coastal corkwoods. Stems are about 1m tall and usually solitary.

***ROMULEA BULBOCODIUM*, Romulea,** Rómulea.

Description: Small, slender herbs with corms. Leaves very narrow and grooved, about 20-25cm or more long, arching. Flowers opening in the sun, varying in size (2-3cm wide) and colour from nearly white or pale pink-lilac to deep lilac; all have two papery bracts (spathes) below the flower, which is short-lived and either solitary or several coming out together.

Flowering: January to March, to April in the hills.

Habitat: Sandy or heavy rocky soil, open places or in light woods, coastal, very common.

Distribution: Mediterranean area, Portugal.

Family: Iris family, Iridaceae.

Notes: Could be mistaken for a small *Crocus* but does not have the deep green leaves with the central white line. The flowers open with a short stem; this increases as the flower matures, so that by the time there is a seedhead there is a long stalk which bends over reaching the ground and the dispersal of its seed is well away from the parent plant. This results in large patches, an attractive sight when in flower.

211

ROMULEA CLUSIANA, Large Romulea.

Description: Similar to *R. bulbocodium* (p.211) but with longer leaves, and flowers which are about 3-5cm wide; the colour, though also variable, has a well-defined orange throat; purplish-pink above.

Flowering: January to February, occasionally to March.

Habitat: In the deep sand behind beaches, always coastal; commonest in the Algeciras and Tarifa coasts.

Distribution: Southwest Spain, Portugal.

Family: Iris family, Iridaceae.

Notes: Usually considered a variety of R. *bulbocodium*, but a recent Spanish work (*Flora Vascula de Andalucía Occidental, Vol. 3*) treats it as a distinct species. As recently as 1970 the large area of sand between Spain and Gibraltar was a spectacular sight during January and February with thousands of these flowers.

BRIZA MAXIMA, **Large Quaking Grass,** Bailarines, Cedacillo grande.

Description: Slender annual to about 45cm in height but in dry soil much shorter, many growing together. Spikelets drooping from thin stalks are pale chaff-coloured but in some the basal glumes of the spikelets are violet.

Flowering: April to June, with old heads remaining until late summer.

Habitat: Sandy and damp grassy places, edges of woods, fields, pathsides, etc., common in southern Spain.

Distribution: Throughout the Mediterranean but spread to cooler Europe by cultivation and as far as New Zealand.

Family: Grass family, Gramineae (Poaceae).

Notes: One of the most charming of the Mediterranean spring grasses, it is much larger than the Common Quaking Grass of cooler Europe. The heads dry well for flower arrangements.

STIPA TENACISSIMA, **Esparto Grass,** Esparto común.

Description: Robust perennial grass forming a large tussock. Leaves tough, long, narrow and rolled; about 3mm wide. Flower stems about 1-2 metres tall; non-flowering shoots with woolly hairs and ligules with short hairs; flower panicles several, erect and dense, 25-30cm long.

Flowering: About April to July.

Habitat: Arid ground and rocky mountain slopes, commonly above 300m.

Distribution: Spain, Portugal, North Africa.

Family: Grass family, Gramineae (Poaceae).

Notes: One of our largest grasses with extremely tough leaves, which were used in the past in country industry for making hard-wearing mats; plaited for ropes and for shoe soles, men sitting by the tussocks doing this work. Another tussock grass of similar height is S. *gigantea* and they often grow together; it has a much more open head.

CHAMAEROPS HUMILIS, **Dwarf Fan Palm;** Palmito común, Datiles de perro.

Description: Dwarf palm often fruiting when stemless but does develop a trunk 2.5m or more if left undisturbed. Leaves in a fan (leaf segments from a central point on stem), stem spiny. Flowers pale yellow, very small in a loosely branched head. Fruit green at first, ripening orange, becoming fleshy.

Flowering: About March to June; fruits ripening from about June to October, remaining on the plant unless eaten by animals.

Habitat: In dry rocky ground and on cliffsides, uncultivated fields and often amongst low shrubs in poor soil; from coast to at least 1,000m; very common.

Distribution: West Mediterranean area, Portugal, North Africa.

Family: Palm family, Palmae (Arecaceae).

Notes: Fans are made from the leaves using new fronds. It is a useful plant to country people with its strong fibres; fruits are rich in butyric acid which causes fermentation. Regrettably, the central growing point is cut and sold in country markets. This is rightly called Millionaire's Salad, as it kills the plant.

***ARISARUM VULGARE* ssp. *SIMORRHINUM*,** **Friar's Cowl,** Candilejos.

Description: A small arum with a tuber, small and more or less horizontal. Leaves dark green on stalks up to 30cm but frequently much smaller. Flowers on erect and rounded speckled stalks shorter than the leaves. The spathe, hood-like, which encloses the flowers in arums, may be brownish-red, white-striped or almost all green. There are several sub-species in southern Spain.

Flowering: November to February and later in the hills.

Habitat: Abundant in open places, hedgerows, light woods to rocky crevices in the hills. Sometimes a pest in new gardens.

Distribution: A widespread plant especially in the Mediterranean and Portugal.

Family: Cuckoo-pint family, Araceae.

Notes: The little hooded flowers are attractive in a vase, but soon produce a strong and most unpleasant smell. Most parts poisonous but tubers and leaves have been used in Spain in the past for medicine.

ANACAMPTIS PYRAMIDALIS, **Pyramid Orchid,** Orquidea piramidal.

Description: One long, thin stem, about 20 to 75cm high. Leaves, the lower up to 25cm long, narrow; those above shorter, some so short as to resemble bracts. Flowers many in a short condensed head about 2-8cm long, occasionally white; spur from base of each flower, very thin.

Flowering: April to July, depending on altitude and winter humidity.

Habitat: In open places in long grass or amongst short scrub, often on sloping ground; solitary or a few together.

Distribution: West, central and southern Europe, including the Mediterranean area; North Africa.   In southern Spain usually in the hills and mountains, rarely sea level.

Family: Orchid family, Orchidaceae.

Notes: More easily identified than most of our orchids. There is only one species in Europe which is divided into some sub-species. The typical form is in southern Spain and is written *Anacamptis pyramidalis* ssp. *pyramidalis.* At the back of the lip there are two projections like tiny parallel walls. These guide an insect towards the pollen at the back of the flower and are called "guide-plates".

***BARLIA ROBERTIANA*, Giant Orchid, Hyacinth Orchid,** Orquidea.

Description: Stout orchid with one thick stem to about 70cm. Leaves, the lower large to about 8cm wide, spreading; the upper erect on the stem, smaller and narrower. Flowers in a heavy-looking head, pleasantly scented; pink with purple, green and white.

Flowering: February to May.

Habitat: Grassy slopes, light woodlands and amongst short shrubs usually in hills and mountains. Typically solitary and not common, but scattered throughout our area. Occasionally low altitudes, but more frequently 500-1,000m. Loam or limestone.

Distribution: Mediterranean area, Portugal, once widespread.

Family: Orchid Family, Orchidaceae.

Notes: One of our largest orchids, not easily mistaken for any other except perhaps the Lizard Orchid and that has the lip elongated into a ribbon-like appendage. In old books the Giant Orchid is called either *Himantoglossum longibracteatum* or *Barlia longibracteata.*

HIMANTOGLOSSUM HIRCINUM, **Lizard Orchid,** Orquidea.

Description: Large orchid growing to about 90cm high. Leaves alternate from the base, large, about 3cm wide and 15cm long. Flowers 50-70 in a long open spike; each flower with a distinctively elongated central lobe to the lip variable in length and colour, but narrow and twisted; flowers with an animal smell of goat; flowerheads vary from predominately cream, brown and green, to pink and brown with less green.

Flowering: May to July.

Habitat: Mainly in limestone areas and often in shade of tall trees but also on sunny grassy slopes in rocky ground, apparently needing good drainage. Local in hills and mountains to about 1,000m.

Distribution: Throughout much of Europe, mainly Mediterranean countries, but also in the Netherlands and Britain.

Family: Orchid family, Orchidaceae.

Notes: Never very common and now becoming rare in southern Spain. It appears to be sensitive to disturbance and where there were several plants growing under some pinewoods on the Sierra Blanca behind Marbella, this has become a popular picnic place and the orchids have disappeared. The colour of the orchid in the plate is less common in our area than the cream and brown form.

OPHRYS LUTEA, **Yellow Bee Orchid,** Flor de abeja amarillo.

Description: About 10-30cm tall, erect, usually several together. Leaves; basal largest in a rosette which are mainly dead by flowering time; stem leaves alternate, pointed, widest at base. Flowers in an open spike, about 6-8.

Flowering: Late February to June.

Habitat: Damp grassy banks and fields, open places, preferring limestone; from lowlands to hills and mountains.

Distribution: Widely distributed in the Mediterranean countries, Portugal, North Africa. Throughout southern Spain but rarer in the southwest, except in Gibraltar.

Family: Orchid family, Orchidaceae.

Notes: A conspicuous orchid with several sub-species, but probably only one here. It is often found with the limestone loving Mirror Orchid (O. *speculum*), an attractive dark flower with a shining blue centre and fringed edges. Orchids are remarkable for their highly developed methods of ensuring cross fertilisation. In some species of *Orphrys*, for instance, the flowers resemble a bee so closely that a male bee tries to fertilise it and gets covered in pollen, this is rubbed off on the next blossom - which is just what the plant wants.

OPHRYS SCOLOPAX, **Woodcock Orchid,** Orquidea de Chocha.

Description: Erect rather slender orchid, about 30-40cm high when in flower but occasionally shorter. Basal leaves wide, pointed, pale green. Flowers variable in colour and pattern but mainly with the 3 outer "petals" (tepals) pink with a green central stripe, but the 2 inner, smaller and narrower, are all pink; the large lip (labellum) is usually dark red or purplish with a varying pale cream pattern often in the form of an "H"; the base of the labellum may be pale yellowish with an upturned knob.

Flowering: Commonly from March to May, June in the mountains.

Habitat: In basic soils and rubble from hill or pathsides, often in dryish places and also amongst low shrubs. Frequent but usually only one or two together.

Distribution: Southern Europe; in southern Spain from coast to at least 1,000m., scattered throughout.

Family: Orchid family, Orchidaceae.

Notes: Could be mistaken for the Early and the Late Spider Orchids (O. *sphegodes* and O. *fuciflora*) or even the Bee Orchid (O. *apifera*). They are difficult to sort out, but should not be picked for later identification. If they do not complete their floral cycle the tubers tend to die and there will be no seed for re-population.

221

OPHRYS TENTHREDINIFERA, **Sawfly Orchid,** Orquidea.

Description: Rather tall, 15-45cm or more. Leaves basal in a rosette, ovate, pointed, upper stem leaves narrow and erect. Flowers variable in colour, upper 3 perianth segments bright pink to almost white; lip-centre velvety and the dark part, as well as the yellow margin, varying in shape and width; base of lip with a small portion usually doubled up.

Flowering: February to April.

Habitat: Locally frequent, usually in basic soils, dry grassy fields and banks amongst bushes.

Distribution: Mediterranean countries, Portugal. In southern Spain from lowlands to hills.

Family: Orchid family, Orchidaceae.

Notes: Usually the first orchid to flower. Pure white forms seem to be fairly common.

***ORCHIS CORIOPHORA*, Bug Orchid,** Orquidea.

Description: Stem one, erect about 15 to 30cm high. Leaves, basal more or less erect, narrow and gradually tapered to a point; those on the stem above, short and sheathing. Flowers scented, in a longish head but variable in length, not dense nor round (see Pyramid Orchid p.217); colour pale to deep pink or even reddish, with varying amounts of green on lip and hood; spur (at back of flower) blunt, directed downwards and slightly curved; lip longer than wide, lobed.

Flowering: April to June.

Habitat: Coastal consolidated sand to mountains in damp meadows especially in limestone areas, less commonly in poor soil, in open areas usually grassy places.

Distribution: Widespread throughout most of Europe (excluding British Isles); North Africa, West Asia.

Family: Orchid family, Orchidaceae.

Notes: Variable in colour and scent and divided into several sub-species; the typical form has unpleasantly scented flowers but ssp. *fragrans*, which is our common form, has a sweet scent. Plants are frequently solitary but grow in large clumps in stable and grassed ground at the edge of coastal pinewoods in Cadiz province.

ORCHIS ITALICA, **Italian Orchid, Naked Man,** Orquidea.

Description: Stem 20-40cm high; 5-8 leaves in a basal rosette, long and with very wavy margins. Flowers many, at first in a conical spike, maturing into a rounded head; flowers deeply cut into long narrow and flat lobes with a hood lined with darker pink.

Flowering: March to May.

Habitat: Grassy banks, light woods or thickets; lowlands to at least 1,000m.

Distribution: Much of the Mediterranean area (but not France), Portugal, North Africa.

Family: Orchid family, Orchidaceae.

Notes: Easily identified by its leaves and there is only one other species of *Orchis* with flowers like little demons and that is the Monkey Orchid (O. *simia*) which seems to be rather rare in our area, but is also in North Africa. The leaves are shorter and widest near the apex and margins are not wavy; lobes of the flowers are purplish and bent upwards, resembling hands and feet. The flowerhead is elongated. There is one other that has these curious flowers, the Soldier Orchid (O. *militaris*) which may not come into our area except in the high mountains. It has a long head, not dense, and the flower has thick legs like pantaloons.

ORCHIS PAPILIONACEA**, Mediterranean Butterfly Orchid,**
Orquidea.

Description: Plant erect, about 20 to 40cm tall, either solitary
or in clumps of 5-8. Leaves in basal rosette narrow and pointed
and sheathing on stem. Flowers in a comparatively roundish and
loose head of large flowers; lip with same colour as other parts
or slightly paler; dark veins conspicuous.

Flowering: March to June.

Habitat: Locally frequent here from about 500m in grassy
open places in limestone areas. Also in acid soils in lowlands;
rarer in southwest.

Distribution: Throughout Mediterranean Europe
(comprising several sub-species). Portugal, North Africa.

Family: Orchid family, Orchidaceae.

Notes: Possibly the most striking of the common orchids here.

SERAPIAS CORDIGERA, **Large Tongue Orchid,** Serapia.

Description: Plant erect, commonly about 20cm tall, either solitary or a few together. Leaves narrow, pointed. Flowers to about 10 on the spike, but with only a few out at a time; lip of each about 2-4.5cm long.

Flowering: March to June.

Habitat: In light woods, damp grassy fields, semi-shade and stream margins in southwest in Cork and deciduous Oak woods.

Distribution: South and west Mediterranean countries, Portugal, North Africa.

Family: Orchid family, Orchidaceae.

Notes: Easily distinguished from other species of *Serapias* here which have smaller and narrower lips that are not as rough. White forms of S. *cordigera* occur throughout.

SPIRANTHES SPIRALIS, **Lady's Tresses,** Orquidea.

Description: Erect one-stemmed orchid commonly 10-25cm high. Leaves (basal) in a rosette but usually dead at flowering; stem leaves about 1-2cm long, narrow, lying against the stem. Flowers white in one row but spirally arranged, each one not more than 8mm long; strongly scented at night.

Flowering: October to December.

Habitat: Grassy fields by and in slow-flowing, small streams; in sand or loam, locally frequent, lowlands to hills but some years missing flowering if no autumn rains.

Distribution: Southwest and central Europe.

Family: Orchid, Orchidaceae.

Notes: New basal leaves appear after flowering. In the background, the little pink flower is *Merendera filifolia* which grows in large patches in uncultivated bare fields where grasses have not yet started their winter growth. (These plants were cultivated from the wild in a garden in southwest Spain and photographed in October.)

LIST OF BOTANICAL NAMES OF SPECIES
WITH AUTHORS

ACANTHACEAE
   Acanthus mollis L.
APIACEAE (see UMBELLIFERAE)
APOCYNACEAE
   Nerium oleander L.
   Vinca difformis Pourret
   V. major L.
   V. minor L.
ANACARDIACEAE
   Pistacia lentiscus L.
   P. terebinthus L.
   P. vera L.
ARISTOLOCHIACEAE
   Aristolochia baetica L.
BORAGINACEAE (BORRAGINACEAE)*
   Anchusa azurea Miller
   Borago officinalis L.
   Cerinthe gymnandra Gasparr.
   C. major L.
   Echium albicans Lag & Rodr.
   E. asperrimum Lam.
   E. boissieri Steudel
   E. plantagineum L.
   E. vulgare L.
   Lithodora diffusa (Lag.) I.M.J.
   L. fruticosa (L.) Grisb.
   Omphalodes brassicifolia (Lag.) Sweet.
   O. commutata G. Lopez
BRASSICACEAE (See CRUCIFERAE)
CAMPANULACEAE
   C. mollis L.
   C. specularioides Cosson
   C. velutina Desf.
   Trachelium caerulelum L.

CAPPARIDACEAE
    Capparis ovata Desf.
    C. spinosa L.
CAPRIFOLIACEAE
    C. arborea Boiss.
    C. xylosteum L.
CARYOPHYLLACEAE
    Arenaria aggregata (L.) Loisel
    A. tetraquetra L.
    Cerastium boissieri Gren.
    C. gibraltaricum Boiss.
    Dianthus broteri Boiss. & Reuter
    D. hispanicus Asso
    Paronychia capitata (L.) Lam.
    Silene andryalifolia Pomel
    S. nutans L.
    S. pseudovelutina Rothm.
    S. psammitis Link ex Spreng.
    Spergularia rubra (L.) J. & C. Presl
    S. rubra ssp. longipes (Lange) Briq.
CISTACEAE
    Cistus albidus L.
    C. crispus L.
    C. ladanifer L.
    C. laurifolia L.
    C. salvifolius L.
    Halimium halimifolium (L.) Willk.
    Helianthemum appeninum (L.) Miller
COMPOSITAE (ASTERACEAE)*
    Anacyclus clavatus (Desf.) Pers.
    A. radiatus Loisel
    Andryala integrifolia L.
    Arctotheca calendula (L.) Levyns
    Asteriscus aquaticus (L.) Less.
    A. maritimus (L.) Less.
    Atractylis gummifera L.
    Bellis annua L.

B. perennis L.

B. rotundifolia (Desf.) Boiss. & Reuter

B. sylvestris Cyr.

Calendula arvensis L.

C. suffruticosa Vahl

c. syffruticosa ssp, tomentosa Nurb.

Carlina racemosa L.

Carthamus arborescens L.

Centaurea conifera L.

C. pullata L.

Chamaeleon gummifer (L.) Cass.

Chamaemelum fuscatum (Brot.) Vasc.

Chrysanthemum coronarium L.

Cirsium echinatum (Desf.) DC.

C. giganteum (Desf.) Sprengel

C. scabrum (Poiret) Bonnet & Barratt

Cnicus benedictus L.

Cryptostemma calendulacea (Hill) R.Br.

Dittrichia viscosa (L.) Greuter

Doronicum plantagineum L.

Galactites duriaei Spach ex Durieu

G. tomentosa Moench

Helichrysum stoechas (L.) Moench

Inula viscosa (L.) Aiton

Leuzea conifera (L.) DC

Ptilostemon hispanicus (Lam.) Greuter

Reichardia gaditana (Willk.) Samp.

Scolymus hispanicus L.

Scorzonera crispatula (Boiss.) Boiss.

S. hispanica L.

Silybum marianum (L.) Gaertner

Tolpis barbata (L.) Gaertner

T. barbata var. grandiflora Ball

Tragopogon porrifolius L.

CONVOLVULACEAE

Convolvulus althaeoides L.

C. althaeoides ssp. tenuissimus (Sibth. & Sm.)
Stace

CRASSULACEAE
   Pistorinia breviflora Boiss.
   P. hispanica (L.) DC.
   Sedum acre L.
   S. forsteranum Sm.
   S. reflexum L.
   S. sediforme (Jacq.) Pau
   S. tenuifolium (Sibth. & Sm.) Strobl.
CRUCIFERAE (BRASSICACEAE)*
   Alyssum serpyllifolium Desf.
   Biscutella frutescens Cosson
   Iberis crenata Lam.
   I. gibraltarica L.
   Lobularia maritima (L.) Desf.
CUCURBITACEAE
   Ecballium elaterium (L.) A. Richard
DIPSACACEAE
   Dipsacus fullonum L.
ERICACEAE
   Arbutus unedo L.
   Calluna vulgaris (L.) Hull
   Erica arborea L.
   E. australis L.
   E. ciliaris L.
   E. lusitanica Rudolphi
   E. scoparia L.
   E. umbellata L.
EUPHORBIACEAE
   Euphorbia nicaaensis All.
FABACEAE (See LEGUMINOSAE)
FRANKENIACEAE
   Frankenia laevis L.
GERANIACEAE
   Erodium primulaceum Welw. ex Lange
   Geranium malviflorum Boiss. & Reuter

GENTIANACEAE
Centaurium erythraea Rafn.
LABIATAE (LAMIACEAE)*
Ajuga chamaepitys (L.) Schreber
Calamintha nepeta (L.) Savi
C. sylvatica Bromf.
Lavandula dentata L.
L. multifida L.
L. stoechas L.
L. stoechas ssp. sampaiana Rozeira
Mentha pulegium L.
M. suaveolens Ehrh.
Phlomis fruticosa L.
P. lychnitis L.
P. purpurea L.
Prasium majus L.
Rosmarinus officinalis L.
Salvia argentea L.
S. sclarea L.
Stachys ocymastrum (L.) Briq.
Teucrium fruticans L.
T. scorodonia L.
Thymbra capitata (L.) Cav.
Thymus capitatus L.
T. granatensis Boiss.
T. willdenowii Boiss.
LEGUMINOSAE (FABACEAE)*
Adenocarpus decorticans Boiss.
A. telonensis (Loisel) DC.
Calicotome spinosa (L.) Link
C. villosa (Poiret) Link
Coronilla valentina L.
Cytisus baeticus (Webb) Streudel
C. grandiflorus DC.
C. striatus (Hill) Rothm.
Erinacea anthyllis Link
Galega officinalis L.

Genista cinerea (Vill.) DC.

G. hirsuta Vahl

G. linifolia L.

G. monspessulana (L.) L. Johnson

G. ramosissima (Desf.) Poiret

G. tournefortii Spach

G. triacanthos Brot.

G. tridens (Cav.) DC

Hedysarum coronarium L.

H. glomeratum F.G. Dietrich

Lathyrus odoratus L.

L. tingitanus L.

Lotus arenarius Brot.

L. creticus L.

Lupinus angustifolius L.

L. luteus L.

L. micranthus Guss.

Lygos sphaerocarpa (L.) Heywood

Ononis natrix L.

O. speciosa Lag.

Retarma monosperma (L.) Boiss.

R. sphaerocarpa (L.) Boiss.

Teline linifolia (L.) Webb. & Berth.

Tetragonolobus conjugatus (L.) Link

T. purpurea Moench

Ulex parviflorus Pourret

LINACEAE

Linum narbonense L.

L. strictum L.

L. suffruticosum L.

L. usitatissimum L.

LORANTHACEAE (VISCACEAE)*

Viscum album L.

V. cruciatum Sieber ex Boiss.

LYTHRACEAE

Lythrum junceum Banks & Solander

L. salicaria L.

MALVACEAE
Lavatera maritima Gouan
Malope malacoides L.
Malva sylvestris L.

MYRTACEAE
Myrtus communis L.

OLEACEAE
Olea europaea L. var europaea L.
L. europaea var. sylvestris Brot.

ONAGRACEAE
Epilobium hirsutum L.

OROBANCHACEAE
Orobanche haenseleri Reuter

OXALIDACEAE
Oxalis pes-caprae L.

PAEONIACEAE
Paeonia broteroi Boiss. & Reuter
P. coriacea Boiss.
P. officinalis L.

PAPAVERACEAE
Papaver rhoeas L.

PLANTAGINACEAE
Plantago lagopus L.

POLYGALACEAE
Polygala baetica Willk.
P. microphylla L.

PRIMULACEAE
Anagallis monelli L.

RAFFLESIACEAE
Cytinus hypocistis (L.) L.
Rafflesia arnoldi R.Br.

RANUNCULACEAE
Anemone palmata L.
Clematis cirrhosa L.
Delphinium nanum DC.

D. obcordatum DC.

D. staphisagria L.

Ranunculus bullatus L.

R. ficaria L. ssp. ficariiformis Rouy & Fouc.

ROSACEAE

Prunus prostrata Labill.

Rosa pouzinii Tratt.

R. sempervirens L.

RUBIACEAE

Putoria calabrica (L.fil.) DC.

SAXIFRAGACEAE

Saxifraga boissieri Engler

S. gemmulosa *sensu* Perez Lara

S. globulifera Desf.

S. granulata L.

S. reuterana Boiss.

SCROPHULARIACEAE

Anterrhinum barrelieri Boreau

A. graniticum Rothm. ssp. boissieri (Rothm.) Valdés

A. graniticum ssp. onubensis (Fernandez Casas) Valdés

A. hispanicum *sensu* Perez Lara

A. majus L. ssp.

A. majus ssp. cirrhigerum (Welw. ex Ficalho) Franco

A. majus ssp. tortuosum (Bosc.) Rouy

Chaenorhinum villosum (L.) Lange

Digitalis obscura L.

D. purpurea L.

D. purpurea ssp. heywoodii P. Silva & M. Silva

Linaria amethystea (Vent.) Hoffmanns

L. spartea (L.) Chaz.

L. viscosa (L.) Chaz.

Verbascum lychnitis L.

V. pulverulentum Vill.

SOLANACEAE

Mandragora autumnalis Bertol.

THYMELAEACEAE
    Daphne gnidium L.
    D. laureola L.
UMBELLIFERAE (APIACEAE)*
    Ammi majus L.
    A. visnaga (L) Lam.
    Bupleurum fruticosum L.
    B. gibraltaricum Lam.
    B. lanceolatum Hornem.
    Conium maculatum L.
    Daucus carota L.
    Daucus carota ssp. hispanicus (Gouan) Thell.
    Eryngium dilatatum Lam.
    E. maritimum L.
    E. tricuspidatum L.
    Ferula communis L.
    F. tingitana L.
    Thapsia garganica L.
    T. maxima Miller
VALERIANACEAE
    Fedia cornucopiae (L.) Gaertner
VERBENACEAE
    Vitex agnus-castus L.

MONOCOTYLEDONS
AMARYLLIDACEAE
    Leucojum autumnale L.
    L. trichophyllum Schousboe
    Narcissus bulbocodium L.
    N. cantabricus DC.
    N. papyraceus Ker-Gawler
    N. serotinus L.
    N. tazetta L.
    N. viridiflorus Schousboe
    Pancratium maritimum L.
    Sternbergia lutea (L.) Ker-Gawler ex Sprengel

ARACEAE

Arisarum vulgare ssp. simorrhinum (D.)M.&W.

ARECACEAE (See PALMAE)

GRAMINEAE (POACEAE) *

Briza maxima L.

Stipa gigantea Lag.

S. tenacissima L.

IRIDACEAE

Crocus nevadensis Amo

C. sativus L.

C. serotinus Salisb.

C. serotinus ssp salzmannii (J.Gay) Mathew

Gynandriris sisyrinchium (L.) Parl.

Iris filifolia Boiss.

I. planifolia (Millar) Fiori & Paol.

I. sisyrinchium L.

I. tingitana Maire & Weiller

I. xiphium L.

Romulea bulbocodium (L.) Sebastiani & Mauri

R. clusiana (Lange) Nyman

LILIACEAE

Allium ampeloprasum L.

A. nigrum L.

Asphodelus aestivus Brot.

A. albus Miller

A. fistulosis L.

A. ramosus L.

Colchicum lusitanum Brot.

Fritillaria hispanica Boiss & Reuter

F. lusitanica Wikström

Merendera filifolia Camb.

Scilla maritima L.

S. peruviana L.

Tulipa sylvestris L.

T. sylvestris ssp. australis (Link) Pamp.

Urginea maritima (L.) Baker

ORCHIDACEAE
Anacamptis pyramidalis (L.) L.C. Richard
A. pyramidalis ssp. pyramidalis L.C. Richard
Barlia longibracteata Parlat
B. robertiana (Loisel) Greuter
Himantoglossum hircinum (L.) Sprengel
H. longibracteatum (Biv.) Schlt.
Ophrys apifera Hudson
O. fuciflora (Crantze) Moench
O. lutea Cav.
O. scolopax Cav.
O. speculum Link
O. sphegodes Miller
O. tenthredinifera Willd.
Orchis coriophora L. ssp. fragrans (Pollini) Sudre
O. italica Poiret
O. militaris L.
O. papilionacea L.
O. simia Lam.
Serapias cordigera L.
Spiranthes spiralis (L.) Chevall.
PALMAE (ARECACEAE)*
Chamaerops humilis L.

*Used in *Flora Vascula de Andalucia Occidental* 1987

GLOSSARY

Achene	Small, dry fruit, not splitting open; one seed.
Anther	Part of the stamen which contains pollen.
Appendage	A pair of tiny lobes attached to anthers in some heathers.
Appressed	Pressed closely; e.g. hairs all lying flat on a leaf blade.
Arum	Member of the large family Araceae (Lords and Ladies is an Arum).
Basal	Arising from the base of a stem, leaf, etc.
Boss	A projection, often on a flower.
Bract	Little leaves on the main stem but above the normal leaves and below the flowers.
Bracteole	Secondary bracts often scale-like, below flowers or flowerhead. (See Carrot family).
Bulbil	A small bulb at a leaf base or amongst the flowers.
Bullate	When the surface of the leaf is puckered, not flat.
Calcifuge	Lime hater.
Calicole	Lime lover.
Calyx	The sepals below a flower, either single or joined together.
Capitulum	Stalkless flowers in a head, e.g. in Daisies.
Capsule	Seed container splitting open; dry not fleshy.
Carpel	Divisions of the ovary, either separate or fused together.
Corm	Resembling an underground bulb but replaced annually on the top of the old one.
Corolla	Petals either separate or fused together, forming a flower.

Corona   A circular rim or cup within a flower, but in the centre and separate from the petals.

Corymb   A raceme, but with all flowers placed about the same level.

Crenate   Leaf margins that have teeth which are shallow and rounded.

Cuneate   Triangular to wedge shaped.

Decurrent   When a leaf base continues down a stem as a wing beyond the point where it joined.

Dioecious   Having fertile flowers of only one sex on a plant, either male or female, but never mixed (see Monoecious).

Drupe   Fleshy fruit, commonly with one stone in which a seed is enclosed; e.g. a plum.

Emarginate   Notched at the top (of a petal, leaf etc.).

Endemic   Native to a specific area, not occuring elsewhere.

Epicalyx   Resembling a calyx and close below it.

Exserted   Protruding (e.g. stamens that extend beyond the petals).

Falls   Of Irises; the widest, drooping petals.

False Calyx   Just below a true calyx and usually cup shaped.

Filament   Stalk holding an anther of a stamen.

Genus   Closely related plants within a family (Plural Genera). The first botanical name (at the top of the pages) is the genus spelt with a capital; the second name is the species used without a capital.

Glabrous   Hairless.

Gland   A small cyst-like organ, like a warty swelling, containing nectar or oil to attract insects.

Glandular   Possessing glands.

Glaucous	Sea-green or blue-green
Glume	In grasses two dry bracts which enclose the young spikelets.
Herb	Annual or perennial plants mainly small and not woody.
Hispid	With bristly or rough hairs (see Boraginaceae).
Honey Leaves	Petals with small basal pockets containing nectar (see Buttercups).
Hypanthium	See False Calyx.
Involucral Bracts	These form an involucre.
Involucre	Small leaf-like bracts just below a flowerhead, as in Daisies.
Keel	In the Sweetpea family, the two inner petals come together making a sharp edge like the keel of a boat.
Labellum	A lip. In orchid flowers there is usually one "petal" larger, lobed and more brightly coloured than the others. (See also perianth).
Lanceolate	Of leaves when widest near the base and tapered to a sharp-pointed tip.
Legume	Plants belonging to the Sweetpea family; also the pod is a legume.
Ligule	In grasses, a small membraneous bract on grass stems; also in some daisies surrounding a single flower.
Loculus	The cavity of an anther or ovary. In the Cress family the seeds are housed in loculi, singly or several, in little compartments.
Macaronesia	A term used for plants occuring on the islands of Azores, Canaries and Madeira.
Mericarp	A portion of a compound seedhead, which splits off at maturity, containing one seed (see Carrot family).
Monoecious	With fertile stamen or styles (male or

female) in separate flowers, never mixed, but on the same plant (see Dioecious).

Mucro	A short sharp point on the apex of a leaf or petal.
Panicle	A branched flowerhead as in many grasses and with the flowerstalks branched more than once.
Pappus	A tuft of feathery hairs or bristles on the seeds of many Compositae, especially the thistles.
Perfoliate	A term used when a leaf completely surrounds the stem.
Perianth	Meaning both sepals and petals (sometimes they are fused and not easily separated).
Phyllode	A leaf stalk usually flattened and functioning as a leaf.
Pinnate	A leaf blade divided to the midrib into leaflets (bipinnate is when leaflets themselves are divided).
Pinnatifid	When the leaf blade is deeply cut into segments as in a pinnate leaf but do not reach the midrib.
Pubescent	Softly hairy.
Raceme	With stalked flowers on a central stem, not stalked again; flowering from the base upwards.
Rachis, Rhachis	The midrib of a pinnate leaf or a main flower stem.
Receptacle	The part that holds a flower (between the corolla and stalk).
Recurved	Curved back and downwards.
Scabrid	Rough to the touch
Sepal	Segment of a calyx, often green, sometimes coloured.
Serrate	Leaf margins notched like the teeth of a saw.

Sessile	Stemless or stalkless.
Setose	Covered with bristles.
Silicula	Short seed-pod, not more than 3 times as long as it is wide in the Cress family (Cruciferae). See Siliqua.
Siliqua	Much longer than wide; Cress family (See Silicula).
Shrub	Woody perennial usually low and spreading.
Spathe	A bract, often large and brightly coloured enclosing the flowers in Arums and smaller ones in Allium species.
Spike	With unstalked flowers on a central stem (see Raceme).
Stamen	The male part of a flower containing the pollen.
Standard	Largest petal in a flower of the Sweetpea family.
Stipule	An appendage, often scale-like at the base of a leafstalk, sometimes in pairs.
Stipulate	Possessing stipules.
Style	Usually on the upper part of an ovary (the female part of a flower); on the apex is the Stigma which receives pollen for fertilisation.
Terminal	At the end of a stem or at the extreme top.
Tessellated	Checkered.
Tunic	The outer dry covering of a bulb or corm.
Umbel	A compound flowerhead in which all the stalklets arise from one cluster from the top of a stem (rather like the ribs of an umbrella).
Xerophytic	A plant which lives in dry areas (noun: Xerophyte).

INDEX OF PLANTS in English

INDEX OF PLANTS in Latin

ABOUT THE AUTHOR

Betty Molesworth Allen was trained as a taxonomic botanist. She and her late husband spent many years in Malaysia and travelled extensively throughout the world in search of plants and birds. Ferns were her main interest and three are named after her - in addition to a tunnel in Malaysia! Mrs. Allen has lived in southern Spain since 1963, where she has pursued her interest in wild and cultivated plants, with an emphasis on the wildflowers of Andalusia.

MORE BOOKS FROM SANTANA

The Spanish Property Guide Takes you step by step through all aspects of property ownership in Spain, giving you sound advice and vital information about property and much more. *By David Searl. 272 pages.*

You and the Law in Spain Thousands of readers have relied on this best selling book to guide them through the Spanish legal jungle. Now, there is a new, completely revised edition with even more information on taxes, work permits, cars, banking, property and lots more. It's a book no foreigner in Spain can afford to be without. *By David Searl. 224 pages.*

Cooking in Spain The definitive guide to cooking in Spain, with more than 400 great recipes. Complete information on regional specialities and culinary history, how to buy the best at the market, English-Spanish glossary and handy conversion guide. *By Janet Mendel. 376 Pages. Illustrated.*

The Best of Spanish Cooking The top food writer in Spain today invites you to a memorable feast featuring her all-time favourite Spanish recipes. More than 170 tantalizing dishes are presented, allowing you to recreate the flavour of Spain in your own home. *By Janet Mendel. 172 pages.*

Tapas and More Great Dishes from Spain This striking cookbook is a celebration of the sunny flavours of Spain - olive oil, garlic, fresh fruits and vegetables, meat and seafood -in an attractive presentation of 70 classic recipes and stunning colour photographs. *By Janet Mendel, Photographs by John James Wood. 88 pages*

Expand Your Spanish Tackle the dreaded Spanish subjunctive and chuckle at the same time? You can with this book. The author keeps you smiling as she leads you through the minefield of Spanish grammar. Not a language book in the conventional sense, but it will help you over the obstacles that put many people off learning the language. *By Linda Hall de Gonzalez. 240 pages. Illustrated.*

Excursions in Southern Spain Forty great trips through Andalusia from the twice-winner of Spain's top travel award. This handy guide will take you to the most famous sights and the least-known corners of Andalusia, Spain's most fascinating region. *By David Baird. 347 pages.*

Excursions in Eastern Spain This guide takes you on thirty easy to follow excursions by car all over the Costa Blanca, Valencia and beyond and tells you what's worth seeing, where to stay, where to eat, how to get there and lots more. *By Nick Inman and Clara Villanueva. 272 pages.*

Inside Andalusia Author David Baird invites you to explore an Andalusia you never dreamt of, to meet its people, to discover dramatic scenery and fascinating fiestas. Illustrated with brilliant colour photographs. Winner of the National Award for Travel Writing. *By David Baird. 224 pages. Illustrated.*

The Story of Spain The bold and dramatic history of Spain from the caves of Altamira to our present day. A story of kings and poets, saints and conquistadores, emperors and revolutionaries. The author has drawn on years of rigorous research to recreate the drama, excitement and pathos of crucial events in the history of the western world. *By Mark Williams. 272 pages. Illustrated.*

Andalusian Landscapes This outstanding book of colour pho tographs is a celebration of the astonishing collage of colours and textures in the Andalusian landscape. It captures the charm of remote villages and lonely farmhouses, fields ablaze with sun flowers and meadows full of poppies, the play of light on olive groves and the sun on the high sierras. *By Tim Gartside. 78 pages.*

Birds of Iberia Detailed descriptions of more than 150 bird species and the main habitats, migration patterns and ornithological sites. Lavishly illustrated with fine line drawings and full-colour photographs. *By Clive Finlayson and David Tomlinson. 224 pages. Large format hardback. Illustrated.*

Gardening in Spain Your most valuable tool for successful gardening in Spain. How to plan your garden, what to plant, when and how plant it, how to make the most of flowers, trees, shrubs, herbs. *By Marcelle Pitt. 216 pages. Illustrated.*

A Selection of Wildflowers of Southern Spain Southern Spain is host to a rich variety of wildflowers in widely diverse habitats, some species growing nowhere else. This book describes more than 200 common plants of the region, each illustrated in full colour with simple text for easy identification and enjoyment. *By Betty Molesworth Allen. 260 pages. Illustrated*

Shopping for Food and Wine in Spain Spain, though now an integral part of the European market, is still, happily, a little exotic. The foods and wines you find in Spanish markets are not always what you see back home. This complete guide tells you how to shop in Spain with confidence - saving you money, time and frustration. 176 pages.

Caring for Your Pet in Spain A practical guide written by experts that tells foreign residents how to protect their dogs and cats and other pets from unfamiliar diseases and create an environment in which their pets can live happy and healthy lives in Spain. *By Erny and Peter Harrison. 144 pages.*

Ventas This unique guide reviews 55 great places where you can eat good hearty food in a country setting at half the price you would pay in a conventional restaurant - and all within a short drive of the Costa del Sol. *By Bob Carrick. 144 pages.*

**Santana books are on sale at bookstores in Spain
or by direct mail from the publisher.**
For free cataloque send to:
**Ediciones Santana S.L.,
Apartado 422,
29640 Fuengirola, (Malaga), Spain**
Fax: (34) 952 485 367
e-mail: santana@vnet.es